Heart and Mind

Heart and Mind

The Varieties of Moral Experience

Mary Midgley

Formerly Senior Lecturer in Philosophy
University of Newcastle-upon-Tyne

THE HARVESTER PRESS

First published Great Britain in 1981 by
THE HARVESTER PRESS LIMITED
Publisher: John Spiers
16 Ship Street, Brighton, Sussex

© Mary Midgley, 1981

British Library Cataloguing in Publication Data .
Midgley, Mary
 Heart and mind.
 1. Ethics
 I. Title
 170 BJ1012
 ISBN 0-7108-0048-7

Typeset in 11/12pt Baskerville by
Rowland Phototypesetting Limited
Bury St Edmunds, Suffolk
Printed in Great Britain by
Redwood Burn Limited
Trowbridge, Wiltshire

For all my students and colleagues,
but particularly for Carmen,
who told me about the *tsuji giri*.

CONTENTS

FOREWORD

These essays all centre on a single point—the unity of that very complex creature, a human being, and the need to respect that unity in our view of morals. This is not a remote, theoretical matter, but one that presses on all of us. The way in which we think of ourselves—the picture we form of our essential nature—directly affects the way we live. But academic specialization continually fragments that picture. It has to be somebody's professional business to put the pieces together again. And this is, in fact, the job of moral philosophy. Though it is a philosophical job, however, it is one that has to be done so far as possible in everyday speech. Any technical terminology is downright dangerous here, inviting us to be clever at the expense of being realistic. Dealing with practical choice, we must write, not as shadowy desk-persons, but as the people that we actually are most of the time. The sub-title of this book therefore invokes the blessing of William James, whose *Varieties of Religious Experience* is a splendid example of this vernacular, unsheltered thinking. I am not, of course, surveying moral phenomena generally in the way that he surveyed religion. But I am, like him, stressing both the *variety*—the richness and complexity—of a range of experience, and at the same time the need to locate that whole range firmly in relation to the main structure of our life. Both these things seem needed in order that each of us can operate as a whole.

Some of these essays have appeared before, but I have revised them all and rewritten some drastically to bring out this central theme. The long introductory essay (which is new) states the theme, and explains a number of background matters for the benefit of people quite unfamiliar with philosophy. With them in mind, too, I have kept the two broadcasts ('Freedom and Heredity' and 'On Trying Out One's

New Sword') extremely simple, though I have revised them. People not previously involved with philosophy may like to read these first, rather than the long introductory essay which surveys the state of the art. Three longer papers (6, 7 and 8) were originally published in *Philosophy* and are slightly more technical. But I think they should still be clear enough to the general reader if he has read the first part of the book. Both the last papers ('The Game Game' and 'The Notion of Instinct') have been cut to about half of their original length, not just to save space, but to bring out points relevant to the central theme.

I am grateful to the editor and proprietors of *Philosophy* (the Cambridge University Press) for permission to reprint the three articles from their pages. ('Is "Moral" a Dirty Word?' appeared there in vol. 47 (1972), 'The Game Game' in vol. 49 (1974), and 'The Objection to Systematic Humbug' in vol. 53 (1978).) 'The Notion of Instinct' appeared in the *Cornell Review* 7, Fall issue, 1979, in a much longer version, and the editor and proprietors (Cornell University) have kindly allowed me to reprint the extract here. The two broadcasts appeared in the *Listener*, 'On Trying Out One's New Sword' on 15 December 1977, and 'Freedom and Heredity' on 14 September 1978; the BBC have kindly allowed me to reprint revised versions. For permission to quote from the poems of A. E. Housman, I would like to thank the Society of Authors as the literary representative of his Estate, Jonathan Cape Ltd, publishers of his *Collected Poems* and Holt, Rinehart and Winston, Publishers. I thank Michael Frayn and his publishers, Wm. Collins Sons and Company Ltd, for permission to make a long quotation from *The Tin Men*.

To acknowledge the help I have had from my family and from colleagues, friends and students would require a thousand typewriters and exhaust the reader's patience; my publishers justly point out that books must stop somewhere. I can only say 'thank you' to everyone.

1 THE HUMAN HEART AND OTHER ORGANS

1 The Function of the Heart

If we talk of hearts today, we usually do it only in two rather restricted contexts; the romantic or the medical. A heart is either the focus of a love-affair, or the seat of a disease. These two matters seem widely separated, not connected except externally and by chance. But a much wider use of the word is possible, and deserves examination. When Lady Macbeth, sleepwalking, moans because she cannot clean the smell of blood off her hands, her watchful Doctor says:

What a sigh is there! The heart is sore charged.

and her waiting-woman replies:

I would not have such a heart in my bosom for all the dignity of the whole body.

(Macbeth, Act V scene i)

These people are talking in a perfectly natural way, but one which has become a trifle awkward for us now, partly through sentimental misuse of words like 'heart', partly because of certain changes in the pattern of our thoughts. What they are speaking of is the *core* or centre of someone's being, the essential person, himself as he is in himself and (primarily) to himself. By comparison, both the romantic and the medical aspects of his life are partial and dependent. On the one hand, love affairs do not depend only on certain special feelings, but on the whole character. On the other, someone who has to have a heart operation needs a surgeon whose heart is in his work, a stout-hearted one, who in unexpected difficulties will take heart rather than lose it, one whose heart will not easily sink or fail him. A medical student who, at heart, has never really cared for his work, would never become this kind of surgeon whatever his brains. The surgeon too, on his side, needs a stout-hearted patient, not a faint-hearted one—a patient who will put his heart into the business of recovery. In this wide and still natural way of speaking, the hearts of both doctor and patient form an essential part of the business. Of course one of them may be *heartless* in a narrower sense— callous, selfish, unsympathetic. But to be that, to have any distinct character, he still needs this structured core to his being. It is where his priorities are formed. It is the organized set of central feelings by which he is habitually moved. Hearts may be narrow and hard, cold and flinty, but they are still a crucial element in people's activities.

How then does this centre relate to the mind or brain? Here too we can choose between a wider and a narrower use. We certainly can contrast the mind or brain sharply with the heart, as I did just now in speaking of the medical student. He may have a first-class mind—meaning that he always passes exams well—without any necessary consequences about his heart or character. But that is not the only way to think of the matter, nor the most natural one. When Macbeth says:

O full of scorpions is my mind, dear wife

this is not at all the same thing as complaining about bugs in a computer program. And again:

Macbeth	Canst thou not minister to a mind diseased,
	Pluck from the memory a rooted sorrow,
	Raze out the written troubles of the brain,
	And with some sweet oblivious antidote
	Cleanse the stuff'd bosom of that perilous stuff
	Which weighs upon the heart?
Doctor	Therein the patient must minister to himself.
Macbeth	Throw physic to the dogs, I'll none of it.

(Act V, scene iii)

The *mind* which is diseased is not the intellect, it is something quite close to what we still call the heart. The heart is the centre of concern, the mind is the centre of purpose or attention, and these cannot be dissociated. This does not prevent the mind from being the seat of thought, because thought in general is not just information-handling or abstract calculation, such as computers do, but is the process of developing and articulating our perceptions and feelings. This is still true even if we confine the term to serious, 'directed' thought, ignoring more casual musings:

> But men at whiles are sober,
>   And think, by fits and starts,
> And if they think, they fasten
>   Their hands upon their hearts.
>   (A. E. Housman, Last Poems, x)

Thought is not primarily the sort of thing which is tested in exams. It is the whole organized business of living—seen from the inside.

All this matters because many things on the current intellectual scene tend to make us disconnect feeling from thought, by narrowing our notions of both, and so to make human life as a whole unintelligible. We are inclined to use words like 'heart' and 'feeling' to describe just a few selected sentiments which are somewhat detached from the practical business of living—notably romantic, compassionate and tender sentiments—as if non-romantic actions did not involve any feeling. But this cannot be right. Mean or vindictive action flows from and implies mean and vindictive feeling, and does so just as much when it is considered as when it is impulsive. In general, too, ordinary prudent action flows from prudent feeling, though this is something to which we are so well accustomed that we take it for granted. It may seem like pure habit—until a sudden threat startles us into consciousness of the motive. We are in fact so constituted that we cannot act at all if feeling really fails. When it does fail, as in cases of extreme apathy and depression, people stop acting; they can die in consequence. We do not live essentially by calculation,

interrupted occasionally by an alien force called feeling. Our
thought (including calculation) is the more or less coherent
form into which our perceptions and feelings constantly
organize themselves. And the compromise between various,
conflicting, strong and constant feelings expresses itself in our
heart or character.

   Of course I am not denying that there can be discrepancies
and conflicts between thought and feeling, or between feeling
and action. There can. (They provide some of our most
serious problems, which is why we have quite a good
vocabulary for talking about them.) But they have to be
exceptional. In general, feelings, to be effective, must take
shape as thoughts, and thoughts, to be effective, must be
powered by suitable feelings. Speculative thought is no exception; it depends on the powerful feelings of interest and
curiosity. When we speak of a thought as conflicting with a
feeling, both thoughts and feelings are really present on both
sides; the distinction is just one of emphasis. For instance,
when a normally prudent accountant, overcome (as we say)
by an impulse, blues everything on a wild investment, at least
two thoughts and also two feelings are involved. His habitual,
steady desire for security was borne down by the detailed, but
misleading, calculations which his intellect so vigorously
produced. He did not operate with his normal degree of
organization, but he still operated as one person, not two.
Disentangling the intellectual from the emotional aspects of
this whole is performing a piece of abstraction, one which
needs enormously more care than theorizers usually give it.

2   The Divorce Between Feeling and Reason

Why, now, does all this matter? The unity of the human
personality which I am stressing seems obvious. As I have
said, however, it badly needs to be plugged today because of a
whole web of theoretical habits which tend to obscure it and
make it inexpressible. In this book, my main business will be
with the strands of this web spun by British moral philosophy,
which from the eighteenth century on has occupied itself with
a dispute about whether morality is a matter of reason or

feeling, ignoring the obvious fact that it is both. Its question has been, in Hume's words:

concerning the general foundation of Morals; whether they be derived from Reason, or from Sentiment; whether we attain the knowledge of them by a chain of argument and induction, or by an immediate feeling and finer internal sense.

(*Enquiry Concerning the Principles of Morals* Section 1)

This dilemma is false. The metaphor of *foundation* is disastrous; a building can only sit on one foundation, so it looks as if we have to make a drastic choice. But we don't. Morality, like every other aspect of human activity, has both its emotional and its intellectual side, and the connection between them can't be just an external one, like that between stones brought together for a building. It is an organic one, like that between the shape and size of an insect. This barren dispute sprang up in the first place as part of a wider controversy, which was only less barren because it was more quickly recognized as being merely a question of emphasis— the dispute between rationalism and empiricism in the theory of knowledge. Does knowledge—people asked—depend on reasoning or on experience? Very plainly the answer must be—yes, on both, but in different ways, and the next move must be to go on and investigate these different sorts of dependence. Since Kant's day, this has been fairly well understood as far as theoretical knowledge is concerned. In moral philosophy, however, empiricists have been a lot slower to see that they could not treat the issue as a football match which, by vigorous cheering, they might one day hope to win. Hume's question only makes sense if it is treated as one about emphasis. It must be dealt with by accepting both elements as inseparable, and going on to a patient analysis of the parts they play in the whole.

Inevitably, these are hasty remarks on large subjects. In this book, I cannot say much about the theory of knowledge, though to avoid misunderstanding, I had better point out at once that I am not waving a lone flag in rejecting extreme, dogmatic empiricism as no more sane and workable than extreme, dogmatic rationalism. The impossibility of defending it has been argued by many good philosophers who are certainly the direct heirs of the empiricist tradition in its central enterprise of realism, common sense, and respect for the complexity of experience.[1] Hume's attempt to show experience as a simple receiving of bare raw material unsullied by thought—as a succession of separate perceptions and feelings, disconnected and occurring at random, will not work. He was right to explore these wilder shores of empiricist metaphysic, but the upshot of his journey must be accepted. Experience is not like this, and cannot be so represented. Humean empiricism is bankrupt in the philosophy of science, and that is something which it cannot afford to be.[2] It is also terribly mean and impoverished in the Philosophy of Mind. Hume himself was alarmed about this, when he realized that the self which he was treating as the only solid reality had dissolved into a loose succession of disconnected events—a 'bundle of perceptions' with no string round the bundle.[3] But he saw no remedy, and this impoverishment has persisted, in the form of a strange, indeed paradoxical unwillingness in empiricist philosophers to recognize the ordered complexity of our actual experience. Since empiricism simply *is* an insistence that experience holds the key to all our problems, one might expect it to lead people to want to map experience itself in some detail, and not to be surprised if it turned out to be complex. And it has indeed taken some of its best practitioners like this—notably Locke, Butler and William James. Hume himself sometimes shared their interest, and phenomenology has been the heir of his efforts that way. At other times however, he viewed the inner life with dour suspicion, determined to make this confusing area conform with his demand for simplicity, and above all not to make use of any concept, however obvious, innocent and necessary, which might turn out to provide material for an immortal soul. Twentieth-century behaviourism is one heir of this timid and unrealistic tradition. I shall be mentioning others. In general, the unity of human life is the central theme of the essays in this book, and though my remarks about it here are somewhat brief and dogmatic I shall try to show in them more fully how I understand it and how I want to vindicate it against false antitheses forced upon it by theory—unreal choices, resulting, I suggest, chiefly from controversial bad habits.

3 The Divorce Between Nature and Will

I begin then, deliberately, with a rather simple paper, 'Freedom and Heredity', dealing with the most troublesome and clamorous current form of this old dispute between feeling and reason—namely, the war at present proclaimed as arising between human nature and the free human will. We are called upon to choose between these concepts, to decide whether we are free beings, or members of the species Homo sapiens, with an inherited mental and emotional constitution. But are tomatoes fruit or vegetables? Does a house need shape or size? The two things imply each other. A being which had no natural constitution could not be free; the word freedom would make no sense applied to it. Such a creature would have nothing which it needed to be free to do. And the natural constitution which man actually has is no obstacle to his making free choices, since in fact it is so formed that it commits him to choosing. There is no football match to be won here. There are two imperfectly understood half-truths, both of which in practice we recognize, and which we must somehow fit together. This is certainly hard, because our ideas of freedom and of nature have been developed in different contexts and are not shaped to fit each other. As has long been recognized, very careful logical plumbing is needed to understand free will, and people who want to do it will always have to think hard. But the present controversy does not only flow from this general, long-standing difficulty about free will and causal necessity. It arises because the notion of the will has been fantastically narrowed and isolated, since Nietzsche, in a melodramatic attempt to expand human freedom into omnipotence. For Kant, the will meant practical reason. It was a name for the whole person, considered as a responsible chooser. Nietzsche, distrusting thought, exalted it as simply the courage to pursue one's own desires. The existentialists, seeing that desires are part of nature, and anxious to free the individual from entrapment in anything natural, separated it off from desire as well, and exalted it still further as the seat of pure choice. But choice in this isolation becomes so pure as to be quite meaningless. And although existentialist jargon is no longer specially fashionable, this is still the only way of thinking open to those who want to divorce the essential self from human nature. That self becomes a mere vacuous abstract force without direction. What is missing is the background map of the *whole* self, within which both the natural desires and the shaping will which develops to organize them can find a context. As I remarked when discussing hearts, certain areas within this whole are brightly lit by current thought and intellectually familiar, but the brighter this light is, the darker and more mysterious we find the gaps between. A sharp beam is focused on the body as the object of medical science. This, however, makes it even harder to peer into the surrounding gloom, even at those neighbouring areas of the mind which (as Macbeth saw) must often be understood for the treatment of disease itself.

Elsewhere a different and weaker light (probably pink) vaguely illuminates the feelings, or certain selected feelings. But this is not supposed to be a very complex or important area. And elsewhere again, there looms in the darkness, uncertainly lit in green from yet another direction, a further item called the will. How are these bits and pieces to be connected? The human being who is the object of various sciences seems to bear no relation to the one who feels, or to the subject making decisions, yet he must operate as a whole. We cannot choose between these items; we need a map which contains them all.

Of course the roots of these difficulties are not new. People's understanding of themselves has always been fragmentary. Probably it always must be so, probably it would always be subject to the paradoxes which Pope noticed in the *Essay on Man:*

> —Placed on this isthmus of a middle state,
> A being darkly wise and rudely great,
> With too much knowledge for the Sceptic side,
> With too much weakness for the Stoic's pride,

He hangs between, in doubt to act or rest,
In doubt to deem himself a god or beast,
In doubt his mind or body to prefer,
Born but to die, and reasoning but to err . . .
Created half to rise, and half to fall,
Great lord of all things, yet a prey to all,
Sole judge of truth, in endless error hurled,
The glory, jest and riddle of the world:

(*Essay on Man*, Epistle 2, 3–18)

What *is* new in this century, however, is the contribution of academic specialization to the splitting process. Mind and body, scepticism and stoicism, god and beast, are now topics belonging to different disciplines. Each is supposed to be discussed in its own appropriate terms, and any area so far neglected is suspect; since there is no proper way of discussing it, it tends to look like unsuitable ground for academic consideration altogether. Within each discipline, there is a further tendency to keep narrowing the territory; to be suspicious of outlying areas and concentrate only on things which can be made to look perfectly clear and complete. In any given subject this leads to feuds between rival factions, each claiming to have the right centre. The only remedy for this fragmentation is to stand back and take a wider view of the key concepts as parts of a whole.

In 'Creation and Originality' I begin this process boldly with the most awkward and mysterious case, the will. Those who consider our nature as something mean, limited and mechanical are of course reluctant to allow it any part in the honourable function of creativity. They follow Nietzsche in crediting the unassisted will with the creation both of moral values and of art. But when did mere will-power, decisiveness and determination ever make an artist, or indeed a real moral reformer? Talents are gifts. It is not a deprivation, or an infringement of freedom, that each of us must live as the person he is, with the brain and central nervous system that he has, instead of shopping around for one that would suit him better. (What *him?*) Not even God can invent himself from scratch. The fear of determinism arises largely from people's habit of treating all causes as enemies rather than friends, deprivations rather than gifts. Gifts are *enabling* causes; it is hard to see how we would manage without them. Actually, this non-religious rejection of physical causes in the name of freedom requires a far narrower, more bloodless and ascetic view of the self than does any religion. For Christianity, the true self is indeed the soul, but the body is a necessary and suitable expression for it; the resurrection of the body will ensure that whole people, not just ghosts, inhabit Heaven. For Buddhism too, the soul must find a body to fit it. But those who want to say that heredity does not shape a human personality at all seem to take that personality as something sexless and abstract, a mere standard will which happens to have got shut up in a particular body. What are our talents then?

In this paper, accordingly, I suggest that we must treat Creation and Originality, not as supernatural interventions, but as aspects of our whole imaginative capacity, and therefore of our whole nature. There is no danger in admitting their genetic sources. We need not isolate them as pure products of the parthenogenetic will. In the next paper, 'G. E. Moore on the Ideal' I discuss an equally mysterious, and related, attempt to isolate the power of moral judgement from the rest of our nature.

4   The Fragmenting of the Moral Personality

It was Moore who ruled that moral judgements could not be supported by reasoning, that all argument about them was vitiated by a 'naturalistic fallacy'. His aim in doing this was actually to clear the way for an aesthetic morality, which he thought would be self-evident once the bad arguments in support of other values were cleared away. This enterprise seems interesting, but it was the other which caught on. This was the point when moral philosophers began to make it a matter of professional pride to ignore all direct discussion of their subject. The autonomy of morals must, they declared, mean its complete conceptual isolation. Before this time, philosophers had normally started their enquiries from the mass of hard day-to-day thinking that already exists on moral issues. Even when (like the British idealists) they finally reached conclusions distant from much of it, they thought it their business to show how and why. In the young Moore, however, a quite genuine moral fervour and insight were unfortunately linked with a strain of arrogant dogmatism which led him simply to dismiss without discussion, as bumbling amateurs, all those who did not share his method. And in an age of increasing specialization, nervous academics found it much easier to join Moore than to resist him. They soon agreed that the scope of moral philosophy must be narrowed to an examination of just *how* moral judgement worked in the absence of argument.[4] This narrowing is of course not unique. Any kind of thinking which is vigorously practised in common life—the psychology of motive, literary criticism, the study of small children—presents academics with the same sort of problem; must they take it all seriously, or can they by-pass it? Anti-empirical take-overs are terribly tempting. The contemptuous simple-minded pundit who strides in talking like an astronomer among astrologers is easily accepted. His programme does not have to be very good. It chiefly needs to be anti-popular, to save its devotees the trouble of listening to outsiders. If it does this, it tends to catch on. At this point, the academic himself splits into two personae. As Jekyll, for professional purposes, he now accepts and studies only what the intellectual fashion allows. As everyday Hyde, however, having still real problems to solve, he cannily continues to use bits of all those forbidden but convenient conceptual schemes—Utilitarian, Freudian, Marxist, egoist, Christian, and whatnot—which he has officially forsworn, but which have neither been properly refuted nor replaced by something better. (As a by-product of this arrangement, academic books, which are always written by Jekyll, become very boring.) To sign up for a manifesto like Moore's is therefore to bifurcate oneself as a thinker. It is also, however, to fragment one's subject-matter—the moral personality. If moral judgements are really exempt from argument, then whatever faculty makes them is split off from all intelligible relation to the rest of the character. The point at which this split occurs varies according to which faculty we take to do the judging, and this is the next issue to be determined.

Out of Moore's ruling about the 'naturalistic fallacy', then, arose one of those disputes where academic narrowness produces its own echo, where the joiner who insists that the only legitimate tool is the hammer is hotly answered by his colleague who will only allow the saw. Moore's own suggestion that we directly *see* moral truths like colours was soon abandoned. Morality is, in the first place, far too disputable to be treated like this, in the second it is far too practical. Serious value judgements give rise to *action*—but why should simply accepting a truth have this effect? Perhaps, philosophers suggested, these judgements are not a matter of sight but of feeling. (This is emotivism.) The change of metaphor from one sense to the other is at once attractive. What we see is the same for all of us and may not matter; what we feel is private, and moves us. Emotivism grasps a very important piece of the truth. Feeling and action *are* essential elements in morality, which concentration on thought has often made philosophers overlook. Hume was right to stress them. And today there is yet stronger ground for doing so in the increased problem of disagreement. This has now become so confusing that we welcome any excuse to stop thinking about it. The suggestion that thought is in fact quite impossible on moral questions, and indeed nothing to do with them, has a strong appeal. And the tradition of opposing feeling to reason in moral philosophy made it look plausible. So people readily concluded that moral judgements are indeed just expressions of personal feeling, and that to 'judge' in any stronger sense would be either wrong or impossible. They welcomed emotivism as a way of saying this. But in doing so they often entangled it with relativism, which is (approximately) the somewhat puzzling view that duties bind only in particular cultures, and that their bindingness is actually just some sort of bargain—an entrance fee exacted for belonging to a particular group, and meaningless outside it. A loose and shifting combination of relativism with emotivism gives rise to the way of thinking which I have called moral isolationism, and have discussed in the essay 'On Trying Out One's New Sword'. On the surface, this mixture looks like a particularly high-minded and flexible kind of immoralism, well-adapted to deal with the clashes and confusions of our day. I argue that in fact it is a fraudulent mess. Clashes and confusions cannot be dealt with only by feeling; they need thought, and no culture can be thought about in isolation from its fellows. Liberal principles depend, quite as much as any others, on serious moral judgements, articulated and endorsed, not just by emotion or some other selected faculty, but by the personality as a whole.

This paper is an extremely short and simple one. The three that follow it are rather more detailed. They deal at closer quarters with attempts of moral philosophers, from the early 1950s on, to find a less flimsy, more workable approach to their subject. The background of these attempts must be briefly sketched here. And the story does not take us as far from everyday thinking as it might seem to. Essentially, philosophers were grappling here with the same problem as everybody else—namely, the moral confusingness of our age. Constant change, and the clash of standards drawn from different cultures, bewilder us, sometimes completely. Moreover, the conceptual tools with which we confront this chaotic scene were largely forged in the last century, and designed to be used against a single, stifling, monolithic Christian tradition. (It is remarkable how many people still talk as if this were now our problem.) Dostoevsky, Kierkegaard, Freud, Nietzsche, and Samuel Butler supply us with plenty of arguments against complacent, dogmatic conventionality, but few ways of finding our way in chaos. Opening windows is a healthy habit, but it is not much use when you are lost in a snowstorm. In this predicament, both philosophers and ordinary people tend to swing violently between two opposite strategies. The destructive response of declaring all thought impossible is followed by the constructive one of having another try. Emotivism was essentially destructive. Seeing its unreality, philosophers made stout attempts to bring back an element of thought into the business of moral judgement. But this was hard, since they still wanted it to be detached from all other thought. The dominant picture remained that of a distinct functionary within each of us, isolated in a separate office for the issuing of value judgements. In A. J. Ayer's original, simple, boo-hurray emotivist theory,[5] this person only had feelings, and was interested only in producing feelings and acts in others. In time, however, he became less crude. P. Nowell-Smith[6] and C. L. Stevenson[7] taught him to deal in attitudes instead of feelings. This is certainly an advance in realism. Attitudes are perhaps structured arrangements of feelings; they involve thought and they generate rules. R. M. Hare, seeing how much this mattered, grew bolder still and suggested that this official's job was not to feel at all, but to direct or prescribe actions.[8] The moral judger was, in fact, our will, our power of deciding to see to it that certain sorts of things should be done. In doing this, he could even reason deductively from general principles. But these principles themselves must still be seen as detached from all other thinking. No reason could be given for them, except where a general decision gave the reason for a more particular one. They were seen as pure commands directing certain outward actions. The emphasis on outer action remained, but the line to other thought was still cut, and there was now no mention of feeling. Prescriptivism was meant to succeed emotivism, as emotivism has succeeded Moore's brand of intuitionism, not as a supplement, but as a rival exclusive claimant. This position has many bizarre consequences, some of which I point out in 'The Game Game'. Various philosophers, following Wittgenstein, had invoked the metaphor of a game as an explanation of situations (including moral ones) which were clearly governed by rules, but where it was not easy to see why the rules held. But this metaphor cannot be a terminus. It only raises a larger question: Why do the rules of a game hold? To understand this, we need to ask what need games satisfy; what is involved in being a games-playing animal? This is just the kind of far-reaching and partly empirical enquiry into our nature and that of other creatures which the metaphor had been designed to exclude. 'Prescribing' was supposed to work in a vacuum, to constitute alone the single crucial operation in morality. But why should there be any such single operation?

5   Naturalism and Reductivism

The insistence on narrowing the notion of morality sprang from fear that, if it were more widely conceived, it would become contaminated, that autonomy would be sacrificed. To understand why the philosophers swung their small search-light over the moral scene like this, refusing to spread its beam, we have to grasp the danger which they were trying to avoid. They called it naturalism. It was the danger of distorting and degrading morality by resting it on the wrong sort of arguments, and particularly on arguments taken from the natural sciences. The clearest case of this distortion is one Moore gave—crude 'evolutionary ethics' or Social Darwin-ism.[9] You are an ethical naturalist if you say that 'good' simply means 'evolved', so that more evolved societies—i.e. more civilized ones—are necessarily better than less evolved ones. Or again, if you say that the fittest—that is, the most successful—individuals ought always to prevail because evolution demands it, and 'ought' means something like 'is called for by evolution'. These examples are striking; anyone can see that there is something wrong with them. But actually so many things are wrong with them that they are not very useful; they do not help us to isolate the fault we are after. Evolutionary ethics is an outstanding conceptual pigs'-breakfast, a classic showpiece of non-thought. Every term in these contentions needs defining, and any reasonable definition of the terms will wreck the conclusions. To condemn this sort of ostentatiously muddled thinking is not to condemn all argument from the natural sciences, or from the concept of nature: it is to condemn bad argument. Consider now a clearer case; the defence of Moore's own position about the value of contemplating art and beauty. Is it *naturalism* if I argue (for instance in a dispute about education), that attention to art is very important, and support this view by reference to the facts about the various capacities of children, and about what experience shows us of how people and societies develop without art? Or if I give a similar account of the importance of play? These are facts about human needs, facts which really might have been different. (It does not seem to be necessary that any *intelligent* being would need art, beauty or play in exactly this way.) Experience is required for the understanding of such needs, and that understanding is necessary if we are to build a priority system. It is an understanding, not just of odd impulses, but of our nature as a whole. If 'naturalism' means arguing in this way, it is absolutely necessary for ethics.

The real danger to the autonomy of morals, in fact, is not naturalism, but crude reductivism, and the characteristic vice of reductivism is not its reference to nature, but its exclusiveness, its nothing-buttery. A crude reductivist claims, for instance, that, 'after all, a person is *really* nothing but £5 worth of chemicals.' This sounds hard-headed; besides the chemicals, what else is there? But in fact if we deliver £5 worth of chemicals—or even £6 worth—to an employer, after promising that we will get another person for him by Monday morning, he will detect a difference and is likely to be dissatisfied. He will be so too if we deliver a corpse. This is not necessarily because he demands an extra entity, such as an immortal soul. It is because the word 'person' necessarily means a certain very highly organized, active item, and raw materials are not what it refers to at all. The whole is more than the sum of the parts, and there is nothing superstitious about this. In the same way, anyone who said that, after all, 'good' meant nothing but 'pleasant' or 'evolved' would be grossly distorting language. But of course this does not stop him showing some less direct relation between the concepts if he will take the trouble to make it plausible. It certainly cannot show that the notion of goodness is conceptually isolated from all relations to other ideas. Permanent conceptual quarantine is impossible and autonomy does not require it. It is reductivism that wrecks many attempts to find a 'scientific basis (or foundation) for morality'.

What is a *basis* or *foundation*? The words evidently do not mean here what Hume chiefly meant by them—namely, the essential element in morality itself. They mean something more like an explanation or justification (Hume had this meaning in mind as well, as he shows when he asks how we know moral truths, but it is a different question). A model which naturally occurs to us here is that of the Foundations of Mathematics. These are the logical principles which mathematics must take for granted—the set of assumptions which are necessary if mathematical reasoning is to be valid. Is there a similar set for moral reasoning? Now there do seem to be some forms of thinking which it needs to use. These may centre (as Hare suggested) round the idea of universalizing, of regarding oneself as just one among others, so that each should do as he would be done by. They may also include the larger cluster of notions within which Kant first put forward this suggestion—ideas like responsibility, freedom, rationality, respect for persons, and treating others as ends in themselves. Without these ways of thinking, we may say, there could be no morality. But it does not follow that they alone would be enough to constitute it. Our reason for adopting this way of thinking is certainly not just an intellectual one.[10] As far as mere intellect goes, either calculating egoism or identification with the whole species would do just as well. To think in terms of distinct individuals capable of mattering to each other, and so think morally, we need our emotional constitution too. Intelligent psychopaths who lack normal emotions are amoral; they do not arrive at a moral position by pure reasoning. Our emotional constitution is not revealed by logic. It is a very large and general empirical fact—something which might in principle have been otherwise. The attempt to reduce morality to its minimal logic is itself reductive; it is one more piece of illicit nothing-buttery. Mathematics actually is in the surprising position of having no empirical part, of being essentially a branch of logic. Morality is not. It, like most other realms of thought, involves empirical considerations as well. These determine the detailed forms of thought it needs. In speaking of such a creature as man, it makes no sense to isolate the rational will.

I am suggesting that exclusive concentration on the will is itself a form of reductivism. This may seem surprising, since 'reductivism' is a name usually given to campaigns proceeding from the opposite direction. But the central fault—the arbitrary contraction of scope—is the same in both cases. To put this point in context, I deal next with the more familiar forms of reduction. In ethics, these come in two main kinds—psychological and physical. Psychological reduction flourishes most today in the form which Moore already

concentrated on, namely hedonism, the reduction of good to
pleasure—whether private pleasure, as Freud believed, or, as
the utilitarians thought, the pleasure of the greater number.
Physical reduction on the other hand deals in the entities of
biology and, through them, of physics. Thus, when an honest
man insists on revealing an awkward truth in the teeth of
bribes and threats, the psychological reductivist explains that
(in spite of all appearances) this man is really only maxi-
mizing pleasure—either his own or other people's. The
physical reductivist, however, retorts that *he*—the truth-teller
—is not really doing anything. What is really happening is
just activity in his glands, brain and nerves, or even (still
more bizarrely) in his genes. The trouble with these high-
sounding views is simply their obscurity, and particularly the
obscure use of the word *really*. Do these two views compete?
Or can both be true? Does either eliminate the ordinary
descriptions of the event? What do they actually claim? The
psychological version looks at first like a simple accusation of
humbug. But humbug is only possible where the real thing
sometimes occurs to imitate, and the case we consider should
clearly be the real one. As for the physical version, that
version must apply to both. Real humbug and real heroism
are for it equally to be described as—after all *really*—only
activity in the cells. But this seems idle. The social and moral
descriptions (humbug and heroism) which we started with
still apply, and are still needed, they make an essential
distinction. The physical one which we add does a different
job; it is perfectly compatible with them but it cannot replace
them. What special honour is being claimed for it?

To make sense of the reduction we must drop the metaphysical word 'really' and treat both suggestions as claims
about explanatory power. The idea then is not that we were
mistaken about what happened, but that it is best explained
in a certain way. But to say *best* here lands us again in the
same trouble about competition. Is there (why should there
be?) any single explanation which is for all purposes the best
one? To explain something is to remove a particular doubt or
misunderstanding. And there is no limit to the number of
doubts and misunderstandings that can arise. Normally,
when we say that a particular explanation is the right or real

one, and supplants others, we are taking for granted a definite question which it was meant to answer. We share with our hearers an unspoken assumption about the job for which explanation is needed. This gives it no licence to monopolize the whole subject indefinitely. In the case of truthfulness, it is obscure how physical explanation could be helpful at all. Hedonism is much more obviously relevant. We may raise the question why truthfulness is so important, and hedonism is directly designed to answer such questions. As it happens, however, it is rather bad at answering this particular one. And even in more favourable cases, it usually seems to provide only part of the truth. Psychological reductions usually start from genuine and useful insights, but distort them by wild claims to exclusive status. I discuss their meaning in 'The Notion of Instinct'.

This is the general background of difficulties about re-duction. We come now to a more alarming recent twist in them, produced by academic specialization and imperialism —the tendency to exalt one's own subject as the only explainer. With endearing abandon, Edward O. Wilson shows his flag:

The time has come for ethics to be removed temporarily from the hands of the philosophers and biologicized (*Sociobiology* p. 562). Having cannibalized psychology, the new neurobiology will yield an enduring set of first principles for sociology (p. 575). We must shift from automatic control based on our biological properties to precise steering based on biological knowledge (*On Human Nature* p. 6). Neurobiology cannot be learnt at the feet of a guru. . . . Ethical philosophy must not be left in the hands of the merely wise (p. 7).

Academic imperialism on this scale is a straight bid for sole power. It does not just offer to supplement other disciplines by showing that it can help with certain jobs at which they fail. It writes their distinctive methods off completely. Wilson engagingly reveals what many specialists discreetly conceal— his conviction that actually, outside his own area, no stan-dards operate at all. Outsiders are only 'gurus' or 'the merely wise', slopping around and flying aeroplanes nonchalantly by automatic pilot. In general he makes it very clear that this is

his view of the humanities (history, literature, linguistics,
etc.) considered as ways of understanding the human condition. But about ethics he is still more explicit. He takes it
that the professed business of ethical philosophers is 'to intuit
the standards of good and evil' (*Sociobiology* p. 3) and points
out, rightly, that here they can have no advantage over the
general public. 'Like everyone else, philosophers measure
their personal emotional responses to various alternatives as
though consulting a hidden oracle. The oracle resides in the
deep emotional centres of the brain' (*On Human Nature* p. 6).
The right procedure therefore, he thinks, would be to find the
organs involved and examine them properly in the laboratory.

There are two resounding and extremely common mistakes
here. The first and most amazing is the general one of
suggesting that we ought to take to dissecting our brains
instead of using them, and that doing the first would somehow
make the second unnecessary. The absurdity of this is obvious
if we apply it to any area of thought—say mathematics or
logic, history or indeed sociobiology. But in the special case of
ethics a further error emerges, one for which Wilson does have
some slight excuse in contemporary—or at least recent—
philosophy. He assumes that ethical thought is in a different
position from other thought because it is not really thought at
all but feeling—simply a sounding out of one's responses to
see whether one is for or against something. Now both Moore
and the emotivists did indeed take it to be that. And on this
view the psychology of the emotions certainly is particularly
relevant to ethics. But this will not help Wilson's physicalist
reduction. The psychology of the emotions is not carried out
merely by introspecting one's own reactions, any more than
ethics is. Wilson has no idea at all of the scale on which
conceptual analysis is needed, or the enormous part it plays in
life. He takes philosophers like Kant, Rawls and Nozick,
when they discuss rights, to be simply expressing their own
feelings—simply coming out in favour of certain familiar
positions. It never strikes him that there already exists a most
complex framework of thought, communally evolved and in
daily use, which can go very badly wrong, and which it needs
great care and skill to put right. Philosophers engaged on this
naturally *describe* the framework—make remarks on what the

notion of right or justice which we work with already is, and what this seems to imply—before going on to make suggestions about what is wrong and how we may have to alter it. Many of these schemes or ways of thinking are enormously complicated. Being used to them, we seldom realize this, and are accordingly bewildered when they go wrong. But they do. They will not just develop faultlessly without attention. In fact the amount of work that has gone into building them is inconceivable, and our debt to the people who have managed to set right serious faults in them is immense. The name for what they do is philosophy. Of course this does not mean that they all need to be full-time philosophers. The 'merely wise' (if wisdom is indeed something mere) have carried a vast burden in the business, and for a long time carried it alone. But as both our culture and our thought developed, the problems grew, and some specialized attention to these difficulties became necessary. Socrates already found the problems of his day so tricky that he decided to abandon his profession (sculpture) and give his whole attention to the matter. It is usually held that his decision was worth while. And since his time, things have certainly not got easier. Not to mince words, Wilson's impression that no special methods of thought are used or needed in this area is a monstrous piece of ignorance, as bad as the ignorance of science which he rightly deplores in humanists. That academic specialization makes both sorts possible is a cultural disaster.

Now there is of course another way in which the exclusive reductivist claim can be pressed—namely, the full-scale metaphysical one. It is possible to set up as a dogmatic materialist and say, 'After all, Matter is real. Mind is less real; or perhaps altogether illusory. Therefore, even if other forms of explanation succeed very well in ethics, history or psychology, these explanations are still incomplete, not just in the way in which all explanations are incomplete (more may always be added), but in a quite special way, because they refer only to something which is itself unreal. Physical explanation is the only *real* explanation because only it deals in reality.' But this too is extremely obscure. Metaphysical reductive claims of this kind look like literal, factual statements. But they cannot be so. They do not bring new factual evidence. What they do is, still, to demand certain methods of interpretation. Thus, to continue with examples from Wilson:

> The organism *is only* DNA's way of making more DNA (*Sociobiology* p.3). The human mind *is* a device for survival and reproduction, and reason *is just* one of its various techniques (*On Human Nature* p. 2). 'Beliefs *are really* enabling mechanisms for survival. . . . Thus does ideology bow to *its hidden masters* the genes (p. 3–4).

And more fully—though with a gesture to the more intelligible point about explanation:

> If the brain *is* a machine of 10 billion nerve cells and the mind *can somehow be explained as* the summed activity of a finite number of chemical and electrical reactions, boundaries limit the human prospect—*we are biological* and our souls cannot fly free (*On Human Nature* p. 1). (Italics mine throughout.)

This is no doubt subtler and more ambitious than saying that people are only consignments of chemicals. Wilson is in fact making a perfectly reasonable and important point, which he wrecks by the meaningless reductive claim to exclusiveness. This reasonable point can be expressed by saying things like 'the human mind is a device for survival and reproduction', provided one understands that these are metaphors, and that one leaves out all words like *only* or *really*. The mind is that, among a lot of other things. Words like 'device' and 'mechanism' have a fairly clear and unpretentious sense in biology. They refer simply to function, without superstitiously invoking a planning agent. Remarks about them therefore do not conflict with remarks about individual agents and purposes, and cannot replace these. Our appendix is a device for digesting grass; but we today have no use for it. Again, the eye is, in an important sense, a device for informed movement and so for survival. But this does not mean that it can serve no other purpose. Constable and Rembrandt used it for all sorts of other ends and it would be mere confusion to suggest that these ends were somehow unreal, or that they were illicit and ought to be abandoned. Again, play no doubt has a function. It has been developed among human beings, as it has among the young of other intelligent species and sometimes among adults too, for evolutionary reasons which presumably have something to do with the satisfactory working of the higher faculties, with the need for practice in developing them, and with the sort of social interactions needed in a society which is much freer and less mechanical than those of the insects. It seems sensible to say that this tendency evolved because it had some value in promoting survival—that is, *as a result* of its having that value. But to say 'then it is only a means to survival' would miss the point entirely. *What* evolved was not only a tendency to act in certain ways, but a capacity for delighting in certain things, and thereby of taking them as ends. The ends of art and sport are now our ends. They are not delusions, nor provisional and superficial forms of the real end, survival. And the end of reason, similarly, is not survival, nor reproduction, but consistency and truth. People, even childless people, can die for these things. There is nothing confused in their doing so.

The remarks I have quoted from Wilson have the form of a familiar kind of debunking remark about human affairs, something like 'Jones's political principles are really enabling mechanisms for survival. . . . He bows to his hidden masters in the Kremlin', or 'Smith's school is just his way of making more people like Smith'. Here we choose certain accounts of these people's motives in preference to others. But since there is no competition between evolutionary function and immediate motive, what Wilson is saying cannot possibly work like this—*unless*, as his language constantly suggests, genes or DNA were conscious agents, sitting in some inner Kremlin and masterminding events. Since nobody believes this piece of fatalistic hocus-pocus, what does he mean? The clue lies, I think, in his most mysterious metaphysical pronouncement of all, 'we are biological'. Clearly this cannot just mean 'biology can be done about us'. Physics and chemistry, history and anthropology and linguistics can also be done about us, without requiring that the soul should 'fly free'. But he does not call us physical, chemical, historical etc. Biology has a special place. What this means, I think, is that the essential or real self is the biological self, that what biology tells us about ourselves matters supremely, and is the only sort of psychology that does matter. To make sense, these metaphysical reductions have to be seen as indirect claims about explanation. Wilson's reductivist language takes us right back to the problem of the fragmented self.

6   Inside and Outside

I have discussed the evils of Reductivism at some length, partly because they are really important, partly to make it clear that I do see what philosophers were objecting to in their somewhat obsessive resistance to Naturalism. Undoubtedly, however, they over-reacted, giving so wide a sense to 'naturalism' in the name of autonomy that they were left with an impossibly narrow territory for moral thinking.

'The Objection to Systematic Humbug' discusses one form of this narrowing, namely the sharp line which some moral philosophers have drawn between motive and action. They insist that the business of morality is really only with outside action—or alternatively, that it is really only with motive. This is a fine example of the kind of reductive mistake which has found itself a special jargon today by misusing the word *about*. Is architecture really about people? or about the principles of safe construction? Is morality about acts, or about motives? The falsity of these dilemmas is obvious and the usage stinks. In moral philosophy, the effect is to separate the judgements passed on acts and motives entirely, and therefore to dislocate the inner and outer aspects of life. Recently the preference has been given to the outer, on grounds rooted in metaphysical behaviourism—the view that nothing except outward action is fully real, so that questions about feeling and motive must be secondary. A person, on this view, is (after all) nothing but his behaviour-patterns.

Here psychological questions about the self become entangled with the ontological ones already touched on; questions about 'what there is' or rather about what it means to say that various kinds of things *are*. There is a tradition, going back to Plato, of treating mind and matter as rival candidates for complete reality—of considering one *less real* than the other. Extreme practitioners deny the reality of one or the other entirely. Here idealists (like Berkeley and Leibniz) are balanced by materialists (like Hobbes · and Marx). Descartes thought both contenders equally real, but so different that there was no intelligible relation between them. All these positions are very mysterious. The trouble is that, once you begin to think of mind and matter as distinct things, rather than as aspects of a single world, it becomes remarkably hard to bring them into any intelligible relation. And— to return to my present theme—this difficulty reflects and aggravates that of relating the various parts of the self. Behaviourism therefore is an important element on the scene, and its story is an interesting one. It was originally invented, and still officially serves, simply as a guiding principle of method in psychology. Reacting against psychologists who relied heavily on introspection, J. B. Watson and his followers proclaimed early in this century a programme in psychology which would ignore data from consciousness and deal only with outward behaviour. This policy declaration need not have carried condemnation of other kinds; after all, there could in principle be as many legitimate ways of doing psychology as there are of doing geography. But in fact it was put forward, especially in its early stages, with a good deal of crusading zeal, involving, not just a distrust of other methods, but a metaphysical conviction that their data must be invalid, since inner consciousness was indescribable, unknowable, and perhaps actually unreal. Behaviourism is thus the mirror opposite of subjectivism. Subjectivism, in its various forms, doubts the reality of the outside world and accepts as certain only the deliverances of consciousness. Behaviourism reverses this process. The piquant thing about this antithesis is that both extremes are often favoured by rather similar people and for similar reasons. Both parties want to be tough-minded, economical and realistic; both are suspicious of religion and the subtler aspects of traditional morality. But which metaphysic to choose? Here is another of those numbing dilemmas which I have been describing. Without a proper connecting background, there can be no choice. One must simply toss up. In the social sciences, the choice often makes itself very simply on occupational grounds. A sociologist can hardly be a subjectivist; a subjectivist would hardly have taken to

sociology in the first place. Philosophers, however, have more
positive reasons for moving towards behaviourism. They have
tried subjectivism, and, as may happen with an unreliable
brand of car, many of them still bear the scars. Modern
philosophy starts from Descartes' 'I think, therefore I am',
which is deliberately chosen as the most subjective position
possible. Descartes himself of course did not mean to stay
locked up in the self. He meant to prove the reality of the
external world in such a way as to make it safe for the physics
of Galileo, and so, finally, for common sense too. But this has
turned out a desperate project. Repeatedly, Descartes'
systematic doubt has led its users away from their goal. Hume
pursued its sceptical branch, which stresses the isolation of
the single self, to a terminus in total paralysis and confusion.[11]
At that end lies solipsism, the view that there actually is
nothing except one's own consciousness—and anyone who
can make sense of that is welcome to it. (If he were right he
would, of course, be by definition in a very different situation
from the rest of us. . . .) Along the idealist branch, which
allows many selves, Hegel built on a grandiose extension—
the Absolute—a superself containing all the others. But this
causes serious alarm by its metaphysical top-heaviness.
British empiricism, always wedded to economy, cannot join
the Hegelian orgy; it must take something nearer to Hume's
path. But British empiricism is polygamous. It is also wedded
to science and to common sense, and it cannot finally accept a
notion of the world which is too mean for their purposes.
Economy is an important ideal to it, but it is not committed to
the life of a starving miser. Bertrand Russell was the last great
empiricist who tried hard and systematically to give a credible
account of the world from the subjective starting-point. He
still asked; granted only my consciousness with its sense-data,
what else need exist? His various attempted answers depict a
series of bizarre universes, each stranger than the last,
presenting no foothold either to common sense or to any
science except certain selected aspects of physics. (In particular *The Analysis of Matter* really deserves the attention of
science-fiction addicts.) Now, outraging common sense never
worried Russell. He was content, indeed pleased, to suppose
it unable to penetrate the real world. But science was another

matter. Unlike Hume, Russell had no interest in scepticism as such. He lived in a scientific age and took science very seriously. His failure there marks the end of an empiricist epoch. It is perverse and unrealistic to form a metaphysical notion of the world which is too limited for the purposes of one's actual thinking. Metaphysical notions exist to be *used*. The scepticism which started as honourable unpretentiousness begins in such circumstances to look very much like humbug.

In emergencies like this, the kaleidoscope of thought must be shaken and a new starting-point found. G. E. Moore, in his 'Defence of Common Sense' gave the right shake,[12] and Wittgenstein made use of it to call attention to a new pattern. Philosophers began to look at language. This has given rise to a certain amount of groaning from those who accuse them of preferring to think about words rather than about reality. Whatever their incidental vices, however, the reason for the move is a quite different and completely sound one. Language is public. If you talk, you cannot possibly be the first of your kind. *I* makes sense only by contrast with *you, he, she, it* and *they*. A solipsist could not say *I*.[13] If Descartes had thought about this, he would not have assumed that he must start his enquiry, like a doomed escapologist, from the awkward position of being locked up inside his own consciousness, with no accomplice to release him. If we did start there, escape really would be impossible. But we don't. Those of us who are lucky enough to begin life at all to the extent of being able to talk, begin it in a shared world. Our inner lives, like other people's, occur within that world, as parts of it. From the start, a great deal of communication flows in and out of our various minds unnoticed and without difficulty; we take it for granted. Of course elsewhere the stream can be blocked, and in bad cases people really can be trapped inside their private towers or cellars. Naturally, we attend to such blocks more than to the satisfactory background flow, on the sound general principle of neglecting what is all right. But to do this is to recognize blocks as a special, if common, misfortune, not as the normal condition of life.

The subjectivist philosophical approach, from which so much was hoped, has infiltrated literature and coloured our

imaginations in a hundred ways which I cannot go into here.
My present business is just to point out that, on its own
ground as a tool of thought, it has terrible faults, and has
certainly come to the limit of its usefulness. About the relation
of mind and body in particular, it has produced vast problems
which it can do nothing to solve. That question, then, must be
somehow restated. We must pose it in a way which avoids the
suggestion of a race where two contenders—mind and body
—compete for a prize, namely, the status of reality. In any
decent sense of *real*, both are quite real. And 'reduction' of one
to the other will not help. We are not making some sort of
quasi-physical enquiry about what material the world is
really made of—mind or matter, earth or fire, rock or gas.
That kind of thing must be left to physics. Instead, we are
talking about the relation between two real aspects of everybody's life, the inner and the outer—our consciousness, and
the outer world of which we are conscious, which includes
human bodies. Economy does not call on us to get rid of
either. Since our problem concerns their relation, to sink one
of them will not solve it. Subjectivism, which offers to melt
down the outer world into a relatively insubstantial mirage,
does not make sense for beings like us who can successfully
reach out to that world's other inhabitants by language.
Behaviourism, which offers to ignore the inner experience,
also splits on the rock of language, because speech is essentially a transaction between two conscious beings. We do not
speak simply to our hearer's behaviour-patterns. Proper
speech is only possible where we regard the hearer as having a
state of mind which we address—as receiving and interpret-
ing what we say. (This is why it is so exasperating to find that
one has been talking to a telephone-answering machine.) The
kind of being that can talk cannot possibly be just a mind or
just a body. Neither can he be a mere loose combination of
these, considered as two separate items. The mind is not *in* the
body as a pilot is in a ship, but much more as the inside of a
teapot is inside the outside. The fit need not be perfect—there
are places where the contour diverges quite a lot. But they are
still parts of a whole, and in general both can only be
understood together, by grasping the nature of that whole.
We are not compelled to say 'a man is really his body'. He is

the whole, of which mind and body are equally just aspects, much more like temper or size or intelligence than they are like teeth or toes. Unquestionably this is a far better way to think of human beings as they are in this world, and I do not think that problems about how they may have to be envisaged in the next world ought to be allowed to interfere with it. If there is a next world (a point on which I have no views) it will naturally call for quite different ways of thinking. But in this world, we must deal with a person as a whole.

This, as I take it, is the first message for ontologists of Wittgenstein's *Philosophical Investigations*. And it is perhaps the central reason why, if Wittgenstein had not existed, someone else would have had to attend to language. The second is the better-known point that *metaphysical* language must be examined. It really is not clear what we mean by calling such very general things real or unreal; translations must be given. These two moves together release us from the subjectivist prison and give us back the world. Many philosophers, however, view such largess with suspicion and continue to look the gift horse in the mouth. They see subjectivism and behaviourism as the only possible alternatives, so that releasing us from one of them must bind us to the other. The outer world, it seems, may now be real, provided only that *we* are not present to inhabit it. *We* must be reduced to our outward actions: any inner accompaniment that is conceded must be unreal and ghostly. This discreet and sophisticated form of behaviourism appears in the ethical view which I discuss in 'The Objection to Systematic Humbug'. According to it, morality is entirely concerned with outward acts, and has nothing to say about thoughts and feelings except indirectly as causes of action. I argue that this gives us a quite distorted view of morality. And in 'Is *Moral* a Dirty Word?' I go on to point out that this distorted view is indeed sometimes found in normal speech—but only when we use the word 'moral' and its derivatives as terms of abuse. Morality which is confined to outward behaviour already has a bad name, and with reason.

7 Putting Reduction in its Place

Crude reduction is always exaggeration, and exaggeration
feeds on opposition. When Tweedledee shouts that man is
(after all) only a naked ape, a device for making more DNA,
an economic unit, a pollutant, a set of behaviour patterns or a
consignment of chemicals, he is usually responding to
Tweedledum's over-ambitious assertions of transcendental
status. Once this game starts, indignation and narrowness on
both sides interact and increase each other. Each party is liable
to become so obsessed with the other's vices that eventually it
mirrors them and the contestants become indistinguishable.
But we ought to be looking for the serious message behind the
shouting.

It is, I think, peculiarly unlucky that the arguments for
taking our nature seriously have often of late been put
forward in a crude and sometimes grotesque reductivist form.
As I have just suggested, much of the blame for this lies on the
opposition. From Darwin's day on, people claiming to
champion the spiritual aspect of humanity have been strangely
unwilling to admit quite harmless and indisputable facts
about his natural aspect. Blame, however, is not our present
business. What we need now is to put together the scattered
fragments of the psychological map. The first step here, I
suspect, is to get rid of the gratuitously narrow and crude
psychological notions which have become associated with
attention to our inherited nature. There is no reason at all
why supposing a tendency to be heritable should commit one
to treating it as crude. The facts about our psychological
needs usually are extremely complex. 'Naturalistic' views like
hedonism and evolutionary ethics treat them as simple, and
this is a factual mistake. These views are bad psychology
before they are bad ethics, and the two sorts of badness are
interdependent.

This point about the complexity of natural facts brings us
back to the question already touched on of what a 'basis' or
'foundation' for ethics would be. People who now offer to
supply such a basis commonly mean by it, not logical
principles, but some set of scientific facts—for instance, the
facts about evolution. This is a different usage from that in

'the foundations of mathematics', but it is no less correct. We can talk of a rumour or tradition as having 'no basis or foundation'; this is a criticism of its facts, not of its logic. Actually the word can be used impartially for any badly needed element which seems to need supplying. Now I have suggested that a rather wide range of facts about human needs, and therefore about our inherited emotional and intellectual constitution, really are needed for morals. Intelligent beings with a different constitution might have quite different duties and a different concept of duty; they might even have no duties at all. So we can certainly speak of these facts as *a* necessary foundation for morals. But this does not mean that they are *the* exclusive foundation, because both logical considerations and other facts (for instance cultural or economic ones) are needed too. No simple set would do.

The point of stressing biological facts is to suggest that our nature matters—that it defines our range of choice quite firmly, and must be understood if we are to give any meaning to the idea of freedom. For practical purposes all of us, I think, accept this inoffensive idea and appeal to it frequently—for instance in discussions of sexual needs, or of the natural needs of children. It only becomes a menace when it is made reductive and exclusive. When this happens, good controversial practice demands of us that we should attend to the positive meaning of these exclusive claims rather than the negative one. (This is on the general principle of attending to what your opponent is actually trying to say rather than simply to his mistakes.) If someone says, 'man is only an animal', we should treat the 'only' as a controversial grace-note added for emphasis, and attend to the main point. Man *is* among other things an animal. He can correctly be so described. He could not be a rational animal, or the paragon of animals, if he were not. The question is, what follows from this?

What follows is an intellectual gain, namely, that we can use, in trying to understand him, many very rich conceptual schemes which have been developed for the understanding of other animals. We have to emphasize that they are many and rich, not crude and simple, and that they never require us to ignore the species difference. Reductive claims can usefully be

stood on their heads here to indicate, not the diminution of
man, but the increasing subtlety and power of the life
sciences. Wilson's remark that 'we are biological' can be
accepted if it is taken to mean, 'biology is much more
developed than you think; it can say something, not just about
our bodies, but about *us* as a whole'. And this is true. To
investigate (for instance) the biology of speech is not just to
dissect the relevant hardware—larynx and vocal chords,
cerebral hemispheres and connecting nerves. It is also to
study the function of speech in social life by putting it in a
context of the whole range of other sorts of human and non-
human communication. Only against this background can we
understand its uniqueness; refusing to compare would never
reveal it. This usage is not new. William James said of the
elements of religious experience that 'we are obliged, on
account of their extraordinary influence upon action and
endurance, to class them among the most important biological functions of mankind' (*Varieties of Religious Experience*,
1902, p. 482). This is not reductive. It does not ban or
diminish other sorts of explanation. It supplements them.
Used in this uncontentious way, words like 'biological' do not
lose their meaning, but they do cease to be weapons of war. It
is possible to consider any important human activity bio-
logically—that is, in the light of its function for the health of
organisms and its probable evolutionary history. But it is
equally possible to treat what we commonly think of as
biological topics from other angles. For instance, the course of
evolution is itself a piece of history, and—as palaeontologists
well know—historical methods are often much more appropriate to it than those commonly thought of as marking the
natural sciences. Knowledge of that piece of history is quite as
essential to modern biology as chemistry and physics are.
Here again, there is no football match to be won. All the
disciplines supplement each other; none is king. In the last
paper in this volume, 'The Notion of Instinct' I try to
illustrate this point by showing how a concept which has been
discredited by a reductive use can and ought to be rescued
from it, and restored to a serious one. This paper is of course
merely a set of signposts and recommendations for further
work—some of which I hope to do myself—not an attempt to

mark out a final position for battle. Instinct is one example of a concept which needs imaginative development, but the point must not be reduced to my examples. It is a general one. As I said when quoting Pope's *Essay on Man*, the notion people form of their self is always and in any culture liable to paradox and confusion, because the topic is really difficult and the material so enormous. Heraclitus said, and he was not being silly, that unsearchable are the depths of the human soul. It would be a really wild and paradoxical development if the greatest increase in learning which the world has ever seen turned out actually to make that important topic less comprehensible than it had been before. But it could happen.

2   FREEDOM AND HEREDITY

Most of us don't know exactly what we have got in our houses —nor, for that matter, in our minds. When we spring-clean, we always find things which surprise us. Around the house, this notoriously happens with those neatly labelled kitchen jars which were designed in the first place to prevent it. There is rice in the coffee-jar, sugar in the rice one, while the sugar-jar, as we are appalled to find, contains nothing but three dead beetles. What is rather less well known, though more important, is that the same thing happens with our thoughts. The label on the concept may still be right, but something different has got inside. For instance, some very odd things have from time to time been found inside those two impressive tall blue jars marked *Law* and *Order*, and also in the curvaceous red one called *Art*. Just now, however, I am not concerned with either of these problems. I want to take a look inside that elegant green jar at the end of the top shelf, marked *Freedom*.

If we look in that jar on the communal shelf today, we shall find there the extremely strange idea that to be free is to be indeterminate, that our having an innate constitution would destroy our freedom. Repeatedly of late, defenders of freedom have attacked scientists who were producing evidence that something in our emotional or intellectual capacities was inherited. I speak of these campaigners as 'defenders of freedom', because that is how they see themselves. They hold that these suggestions about our innate constitution simply have to be false—because, if they were true, they would make us slaves. Often they feel that even to discuss the possibility of innateness is so offensive to human dignity that such speakers must not be heard, that to hear their arguments patiently would commit us to political iniquities. Scientists, in replying to these attacks, often have not paid much attention to this belief, because they have been busy in substantiating the particular facts which they have brought forward. But we must look at the interpretation before we can make sense of the facts. People who are convinced that something *must* not be true are in no state to take in the evidence for or against it.[1]

I want to say that those who think they are defending freedom in this way have radically misunderstood it, and can only do it harm. The point is just this. Neither freedom nor equality demands that we should really be blank paper at birth, completely indeterminate beings. What this would be like is not easy to see, but it would certainly not be a state compatible with freedom. An indeterminate being cannot be a free one. To be free, you have to have an original constitution. Freedom is the chance to develop *what you have it in you to be*—your talents, your capacities, your natural feelings. If you had no such particular potentialities in you for a start, you could have no use for freedom and it could not concern you. Neither can a belief in equality possibly be a belief that we are all identical, standard pieces of white paper, equally capable by nature of passing some test or other. Equality is a moral principle, not a factual one, and it means that we all have the same basic right to fair treatment, *whatever* our capacities. The fact that those capacities vary has no dangerous political consequences at all.

The reason why people believe that it is dangerous is, however, a very interesting one, and deserves attention. The inequalities in our capacities really do become sinister if we make a foolish assumption which apparently often is made—namely, that testing people's capacities is somehow a suitable way of assessing their essential worth. All of us have some incapacities. Normally, we are not certain whether these are innate or acquired, and this does not concern us greatly. What does concern us vitally, however, is whether people choose to despise us for them. This can make all the difference to our lives, and it can do it just as much with acquired incapacities as with inherited ones. If the assumption *that contempt is a proper response to incapacity* is allowed to stand, no causal analysis of incapacities will do anything for people as they are today. The attraction of causal analysis is that it seems to make unequal performance removable in the future.

If the cause of all incapacity is social, and *if* social engineering will some day succeed in removing it, then a hope seems to arise that, in a better age, everybody will be able to pass IQ tests equally well—perhaps, ideally, with exactly the same marks. But even if this bizarre hope were well-founded, it would still leave untouched the central error of drawing wrong practical and evaluative conclusions from this testing. Test results are only important if the test is somehow taken to evaluate people generally.

It is surely obvious that this is an absurd idea, one which must evaporate at once on exposure. Even if tests measure natural cleverness usefully, cleverness cannot be a measure of personal worth. Plenty of very clever people are fools, idlers, obsessives, liars, psychopaths or crooks. But the point is more general than that. No other single quality could serve as such a measure either. Personal worth is not that sort of thing. We are simply not in a position to *grade* each other at all. We can use tests only for quite limited practical purposes. Even for those purposes, tests are fallible and often give more limited guidance than testers suppose, because no test can escape the conceptual limitations of its inventors, and of those limitations, in the nature of things, they are themselves unaware. Any talk of testing *intelligence* is therefore doubly shaky. On top of the usual local difficulties about just what kind of cleverness we are testing, there is the fact that 'intelligence' does not in normal usage mean just cleverness at all, but a quality of the whole character. To call somebody intelligent is not just to speak of his logical subtlety or calculating power, but of his good sense, his power of judgement. This is something which involves his whole developed system of priorities. It expresses his general attitude to life and depends a great deal both on his experience and his will. There are plenty of immensely gifted people who are clever fools, who continually make personal and political judgements which are plain stupid. They do not only fail to use their brains; they use them to confuse issues and to defend follies. The phenomenon is common. It is possible, of course, to say of such people that they have an intelligence but do not use it. But this is not the most ordinary or natural use of the term, and, because the word is an everyday one, it is *not* possible to insist on changing its normal usage, just because academics want to use it in a certain technical way.

Of course, psychologists themselves may be, and often are, quite innocent of intending the distortion which their choice of words actually produces. They want to use tests, quite unpretentiously, to do certain modest and necessary jobs—to diagnose subnormality, to detect capacities in children which are concealed by bad or unsuitable teaching, to establish the effect of disease, and so on. And here they may work admirably, without committing anyone to any special view on just *what* is being tested. But the situation thus produced is unstable, because, in our madly competitive age, any test attracts attention, and is liable to get inflated into a general criterion for judging people's personal worth. The blame here must rest, not specially on the psychologists, but on the temper of the age, on all of us. In a socially mobile culture, people apparently find it hard to dispense with the hierarchy of evaluation which more structured societies provide ready-made in aristocratic or class systems, and they misuse academic work to supply it. But once this occurs outside the lab, psychologists cannot ignore it. If they want to go on using the tests, they will have to grapple with the quite hard philosophical problems which they have raised about the relation of brains to character, of knowledge to goodness. They need to think out, and explain clearly at a popular level, why they are *not* divinely appointed markers in a Last Judgement examination on people's total worth. Alternatively, if they don't want this job, they could turn aside from the tests for a time, and interest themselves in other aspects of how we inherit capacity, for instance, in different *kinds* of natural cleverness rather than in different quantities of an undifferentiated abstraction, and particularly in how these different kinds reveal themselves in the development of small children.

It is interesting to notice that, when we consider the education of children, everybody believes in inherited capacities, and that this belief gets stronger and more influential the further its owner stands towards what may still be called the Left. The business of education, theorists agree, is to bring out what is *in* the child rather than to impose on him the patterns of his society. His own gifts must be detected, his natural bent encouraged. He must not be treated as standard undifferentiated material, dough to be stamped into any socially acceptable biscuit, but more like a plant or tree, which contains its own characteristic potentiality, and needs to unfold it. Attempts to force square pegs into round holes will be disastrous (so this very sensible doctrine runs) not only to the peg itself, but also to society, since the natural tendencies are so strong and specific that the moulding attempt can only produce a maimed human being. If we want those around us to be vigorous, capable people, we must allow them to find the life that suits their individual bent, and this can only be done by seeking out and respecting the distinct individual capacities of children. Whatever proportion this principle may bear to the other requirements of education, it is obviously very important, and is to some extent accepted in practice by everybody concerned with bringing up children. Right from birth, they vary strongly, and nobody can stop them doing so. It is therefore somewhat extraordinary that the denial of innate tendencies should ever have got a foothold, particularly on the Left, and worth examining how this has happened.

In recent thought, there are two main sources of anti-innatism. One, stemming from the empiricist tradition, is behaviourist psychology, showing man as infinitely plastic, a passive being, shaped entirely by his society. The other is existentialism, showing man as a pure abstract will. As Sartre puts it flatly, there is no such thing as human nature.[2] At first sight, these two pictures are very different. They are certainly not compatible. But people often oscillate between them, making occasional use of both, because both are expressly designed to exclude genetic causes of conduct. The use, however, has to be occasional, because both views, if seriously thought through and made consistent, are unreal. It is impossible to reconcile either of them with common sense—meaning by common sense, not some special naïve set of beliefs, but any sort of practical assumption compatible with the business of everyday living. Nobody could possibly conduct his life on the assumption that he himself and those around him were just socially stamped blobs of inert plastic, nor that they were just pure, self-creating wills, let alone both.

The attraction of both views in this context is that they provide strong, simple, colourful answers to certain political *misuses* of notions like human nature. (In other contexts of course both have other attractions, but these do not concern us here.) Because repressive and reactionary theorists have often defended their views by appealing to human nature, their opponents want to abolish that notion, overlooking the fact that left-wing theorists need it just as much and appeal to it as often. We shall see this shortly in the cases of Marx and Mill, but the point is more general. The notion of human nature is wide and indispensable to political thought. Thinkers of all colours have always used it, and it is still presupposed by those who officially deny it. It is not clear what is meant by the proposal to operate without it. (For instance, those who deny that man is naturally aggressive on the ground that he is naturally friendly are not dispensing with the notion of human nature.) The real disputes are about what human nature is like.

Reformers, however, like extreme doctrines. Controversy generates melodrama, and a number of them here have fallen into metaphysical overkill. Marx, for instance, sometimes declared that there was no such thing as human nature, only human history. He said this because he wanted people to rouse themselves for drastic changes. But obviously human nature and human history are not alternatives, but complementary concepts. Human nature underlies historical change and is necessary to account for it. When people resist and change the culture they were brought up with, they do so because their nature demands it. Conditioning fails here, because that which was conditioned is stronger than its conditioning. People are naturally capable of demanding and bringing about many drastic changes, and of profiting by them. Any notion that their nature was inert would be clearly contrary to the facts. Marx, like so many reformers, was exaggerating for simplicity. He made simple rulings to keep difficult theoretical points out of his hair till the main issue before him was settled. But if we took his simple ruling literally, if we did jettison the notion of human nature, Marx's ideas would suffer as much as anyone's. It would be impossible then for him to make his great attack on the *dehumanization* of the working class. If we had no original constitution, there would be no such thing as being human. Being human means living in a way which suits our natural feelings and faculties. If we were really indeterminate, any secure way of life would do, provided we were used to it. *Brave New World* would then be as good as anywhere else. We would then have no specific needs, and certainly no need to use our rational faculties, to be independent, to control our destiny. Freedom accordingly could have no meaning for us. As B. F. Skinner has helpfully pointed out, if human beings were really as he describes them, freedom and dignity would indeed be useless concepts.[3] Nor will it help to move to Sartre's position and consider ourselves as pure wills, choosing in a genetic vacuum. Choosing means deciding between two things which you want, and deciding which of them you want most. The wanting must happen before the choosing can begin. But the wanting is a matter of our emotional and intellectual constitution. A being which was all will and no natural tastes could no more use its freedom than a blob of plastic jelly. In fact it is hard to see how either being could ever act at all.

Freedom, then, is not indefiniteness. But the Blank Paper idea of humanity only allows indefiniteness, so it is useless to freedom. This is as true of our emotional constitution as of our intellectual one, but my present business is mainly with the intellectual one—with our capacities, our talents, our gifts. Capacities *are* gifts. Where do they come from? (This is not a question about God. He may well be their ultimate source. But my present question is, by what channel do they reach us?) It will not help to suggest—as Nietzsche or Sartre might —that we invented or created them for ourselves. The power of invention is itself just the sort of gift we are discussing. To invent or create anything, you must already have both very specific wants and equally specific powers. Their specificness is in fact extraordinary. Right from birth, people are individuals; each person is different *in kind*. I think this is in part what makes the concentration on IQ seem so unsuitable and offensive. What happens in heredity certainly is not that we are born with a definite quantity of a standard stuff called intelligence, or even cleverness, entitling us to a particular place in the social hierarchy, a pre-programmed degree in some monstrous cosmic examination. Instead, we each have our own peculiarly formed set of capacities and incapacities, our own personal repertoire. From this flow distinct tastes and powers, which can often startle both ourselves and those around us, which may find no path in our culture, and can appear extremely early. People who have not seen this happening in small children and who feel incredulous about it, might consider the case of mathematical prodigies— 'calculating boys' who have a specific and remarkable talent for problem-solving without training—indeed, training may only do it harm. Related to these, but even more impressive, is the case of certain great mathematicians like Gauss who have appeared in uneducated families with no mathematics going on round them. A striking example is the great Indian mathematician Ramanujan. He, unlike Gauss, did not even get any encouragement from his teachers. He had a very mediocre education which did not even get him to university —so that he had to rediscover for himself a great deal of existing mathematics. Yet he went on to become one of the great mathematicians of this century. This happened *without* favourable conditioning, so it makes no sense to say that conditioning produced it.

The fascinating thing here is not just the capacity, but the interest which goes with it. Our faculties demand use; we need to do what we are fitted for. That delightful wood-engraver, Thomas Bewick, was the son of a small farmer in a lonely part of Northumberland. He tells in his *Memoir* how from his earliest years he used to draw pictures, with anything he could get and on any surface he could find, although nobody suggested this to him and on the whole people discouraged him. 'At that time', he goes on, 'I had never heard of the word "drawing", not did I know of any other paintings besides the king's arms in the church, and the signs in Ovingham of the Black Bull and other inns.'

Bewick, in fact, was a *born* draughtsman, just as Ramanujan was a born mathematician. Such people exist. Therefore, there has to be something wrong with a concept of freedom which can't accommodate them. Certainly, they show that freedom has its limits. Nobody is free to have somebody else's gifts as well as his own, or instead of them. Ramanujan and

Bewick could not exchange careers. Everybody is who he is, and not another person. But we knew that already, and it would be stark madness to complain of it. We are looking for freedom, not omnipotence. Real gifts, in their nature, are limited. Everything real is limited. Bewick wasn't a potential Leonardo who found himself unfortunately frustrated. He was himself. And the world doesn't need two Leonardos, but it badly needs one Bewick.

Now it is exactly this variety, this obstinate innate uniqueness of each human being, that gives real force to the demand for political freedom. Mill, in his *Essay on Liberty*, emphasized it constantly and correctly with organic metaphors. People, he said, are like trees which should have their full shape and not be pollarded; like human feet, which should have their natural growth and not be bound. They don't have a single stereotype, he insisted—and that is why we need a rich, varied, hospitable, enterprising society. But if they were *not* innately unique, if they were naturally indeterminate, there would be no objection to pouring the lot of them into standard moulds. It is quite time that the radical Left got rid of this confusion, this dead beetle which is poisoning its concept of freedom.

3   CREATION AND ORIGINALITY

Inspiration comes from the earth, which has a past, a history, and a future, not from the cold and immutable heavens.

Joseph Conrad, *Some Reminiscences*, Ch. 5.

The creation of moral values is a pressing topic because, whether we use words like *creation* or not, we all need to find new moral ideas to help us deal with a confused and changing world. The notion that these ideas must be totally new, that they should not rest at all on traditional supports, exists and concerns us all. In European philosophy, since Nietzsche, this notion has often been put in terms of creation through the will. In Anglo-Saxon philosophy it has been much more modestly expressed by emotivism and prescriptivism, and prepared for before that by intuitionism. But it seems better to discuss Sartre's and Nietzsche's outspoken, tuppence-coloured version, because it is clearer and more forceful, and is closer to life. As Plato well knew, the tuppence-coloured kind of philosophy is the kind with an influence on life. It inevitably forms the storehouse from which the more discreet abstractions must be drawn.

I take very seriously what people like Sartre and Nietzsche say about the creation of values. The need for real originality, for serious and independent thought about morals, is so sharp that we cannot afford to overlook any attempt to make it possible. I must point out, too, that neither of them puts forward his doctrines in the crude, unbalanced form which my selective quotations may suggest. That crude form is what readers have chosen to notice in their work. Both of them actually balanced it by other doctrines—Sartre by that of *facticity*, or the contribution which culture makes to character, and Nietzsche by his psychology, or as he called it 'natural history', of motive. As so often happens, however, the extreme

ideas caught on and the explanations did not. This is the
penalty of being very influential. But the extreme ideas are
not the public's invention, they are genuinely present, and
there really does seem to be something badly wrong with the
method which both philosophers use of talking about originality in terms of creation and the will. We need to look
closely at these notions, and ask what the metaphor of
creation means here. In this paper I shall attend chiefly to the
obvious religious model, which will give us so much trouble
that I shall not try to say much about the rather subtler notion
of creation in art. The religious model is the original one, and
its oddities are important. This is not, it seems, a case where
the metaphor is irrelevant, and conveys a quite viable idea.
The whole notion of creating or inventing new moral values
through the will is a disastrous muddle. The touch of
megalomania which surrounds such talk is no accident; it
reveals the notion's essential craziness. The human will is not
a mechanism for generating new thoughts out of nothing. It is
a humble device for holding onto the thoughts which we have
got and using them. Kant, in fact, was right when he said 'the
will is nothing but practical reason',[1] thought in action. What
generates thoughts is the imagination. And these new thoughts
that it produces don't then automatically make old thoughts
obsolete. There is no built-in obsolescence for thoughts. The
new must compete on level terms with the old and be
criticized. Without continuity, new thoughts are meaningless
and unusable.

But, in the Nietzschean tradition, the will is essentially a
device for *dis*continuity. Its whole point is its arbitrariness, its
resistance to all explanation. And freedom itself is valued
chiefly in this negative way, as the isolation of the will. This
makes a mystery. We need to ask: what would it be like to
create values? Nietzsche used this notion to make two points
—the negative one of breaking totally with the past, and the
positive one of competing successfully with God, of doing for
oneself what God had previously claimed to do for one. Here,
for instance, at the outset of *Thus Spake Zarathustra*, he shows
man confronting his own tradition:

'Thou Shalt' lieth gold-glittering in his path, a scaly beast, on each scale
there shineth in letters of gold 'Thou shalt'. Thousand-year old values shine
on those scales, and thus saith the mightiest of all dragons; All value in all
things shineth in me.

All value is already created, and all created value—that am I. Verily
there shall be no more 'I will'. Thus saith the Dragon.

This dragon, says Nietzsche, man has to slay, 'to create for
himself freedom for new creation'. For this:

there needeth an holy yea-saying; its *own* will the spirit now willeth; he that
was lost to the world gaineth his *own* world. . . .

Once you said 'God' when you gazed on distant seas, but now I have
taught you to say 'superman'. God is a supposition, but I want your
supposing to reach no further than your creating will. Could you create a
God? So be silent about all Gods. But you could surely create the
superman.

(*Zarathustra* part 2 section 2, 'In the Happy Isles')

The notion of creation is central to Nietzsche; he comes back
to it constantly. But what does creation mean when people,
not gods, are said to do it? If God is really dead, why should
we dress up in his clothes? In Sartre, there is the same explicit
reference to the divine model. For instance, answering the
objector who says 'your values are not serious since you
choose them for yourselves'. Sartre replies, 'To that I can only
say that I am very sorry that it should be so, but if I have
excluded God the father, there must be someone to invent
values'.[2] Now what is this invention or creation which is
demanded? In the first place is it public or private? Are we all
supposed to be engaged, together, on making new values
which will serve the whole human race, or do we set out, each
separately, to make our own private and incommunicable
sets? Nietzsche himself often talks in the first way, the public
collective way:

None yet knoweth, what is good or evil—unless it be that he is a creator!

But a creator is he that *createth man's goal* and giveth earth its meaning and
its future; he it is that first maketh good and evil *to be*.

(*Zarathustra*, part 3; 'Of Old & New Tables')

This is public; it leads him on to the idea of the superman and the superman is certainly a public phenomenon. But, quite as often, he emphasizes the solitude of the individual, as above—'its *own* will the spirit now willeth; he that was lost to the world gaineth his *own* world'. You can't have it both ways. Existentialism splits on the same rock, though it is much more explicitly committed to the private interpretation.

Public or private, however, what does *creation* mean? The most obvious sense of the word is the strong one, the big bang, the original making of the world by God. There are other, weaker senses, which I shall look at later. But both Sartre and Nietzsche make it clear that the strong sense is the one they want, and back it with the explicit religious reference; man is God's successor:

In man, *creature* and *creator* are united; in man there is matter, fragment, excess, clay, mud and madness; but in man there is also creator, sculptor, the hardness of the hammer, the divine spectator and the seventh day—do you understand this antithesis?

(*Beyond Good and Evil*, sec. 225, see also 260–261)

Now there are two very odd points about this comparison. First, God's creation is a once-for-all job; if it is a Big Bang, it admits of no afterthoughts. (A God who keeps absent-mindedly adding a pear-tree here, a hippopotamus there, shows himself to have been an incompetent creator in the first place.) So, if the comparison works out, the idea should not be that we may, any of us, add a value now and then to a universe which is already a going concern, but rather perhaps that we each create our own whole universe? It is fairly hard to find a sense for this. It seems to demand solipsism. Second, God's creation is, if taken seriously, a very mysterious affair indeed—so mysterious as to throw little light on its analogue in man. The main point of saying that God did it is indeed to express that we cannot at all think how it was done (as the Book of Job points out). The comparison with *making* which is certainly present shows God as like a human craftsman, except that he just happens to be able to work instantly and without tools or raw materials, or at least with none that we can at all understand. But this is a sort of making which we know nothing about. The point then of bringing in talk of creation for values (as for art) must be mainly the negative one of saying that we don't understand how it is done. But people who urge us to do it have to conceive it as possible; the mysteriousness of the idea is not meant as a discouragement.

It will be natural to suggest here that we aren't actually being asked to create the whole world, only the values for it. *But to add the values when you have done the creating is to have an afterthought—and a quite incoherent one.*

It is worth noting that the special job of creating values is not in fact attributed to God by the writer of Genesis (nor by any other creation scripture that I have ever heard of). In Genesis, God looks at each day's work when he has finished it and *sees* that it is good; then finally:

God saw everything that he had made, and behold it was very good.
(Genesis 1.31)

(He might perhaps have been reading G. E. Moore, but not Nietzsche.)

If creating values means making things be good which otherwise would not be—putting goodness into them separately by an act of the will—this is no part of God's work, and is altogether a pretty obscure idea. For a creator, it seems to fall into a much worse class of afterthought than adding a hippopotamus. To create an organism properly is to create its 'values'. You cannot have a plant or animal without certain quite definite things being good and bad for it. To make a change in them would be to alter the creature itself. Changes of this sort happen all right in the course of evolution, but they happen through adaptation; they don't need any special creation and they depend on nobody's will. When a fish in the Australian desert becomes adapted to hot salt water, then hot salt water is good for it and cold fresh water would be bad; to change that set up you would have to change the fish. In just the same way, when human beings have evolved the emotional constitution that they now have, it will be no good willing it to be good for them (for instance) to lose all interest in the tie between particular parents and children (as Plato proposed in *The Republic*),[3] or to talk only to exchange information, or to mate as chimpanzees do, without any social consequences whatever, or to tolerate any level of overcrowding. Proposing to make these things good by an act of the will is nonsense. Each creature has its own faculties and not others. And as Aristotle pointed out,[4] for each creature it must be good to use its faculties and bad to be prevented from doing so. Things needed for the use of its faculties therefore *are* good. And these faculties depend on inheritance, not on the will.

This sort of biological context is the normal, regular, intelligible 'source' of values. What is valuable for a given species is *not* a contingent matter except to people who know nothing of that species.

I have been suggesting that talk of *creating values* through the will involves making men ape God, and indeed *outdo* God, making them do something incoherent which it makes little sense to talk even of God as doing. But apart from this and more generally, it is thoroughly objectionable as far as I can see for people who don't believe in God to invoke God's supposed behaviour to explain man's. What sort of explanation can it give? If the idea of God is to go, it goes because it is unintelligible and unnecessary. It must then surely take with it the whole system of concepts designed for God's special position. If there is nothing which is *omnipotent*, *omniscient*, *omnipresent*, and so forth then there is nothing which can, in this strong sense, *create*. Once more, if God is dead, why dress up in his clothes? Very interestingly, Nietzsche does give a reason, and it is simply a psychological excuse. It is his feeling of guilt:

God is dead. God remains dead. And we have killed him. How shall we console ourselves, the most murderous of all murderers?
. . . Is not the magnitude of this deed too great for us? Shall we not ourselves have to become gods merely to seem worthy of it?
(*The Joyful Wisdom*, 125—from the profound and impressive Madman's Speech.)

In the Introduction to the same book, he wrote:

Doubt devours me. I have killed the law, and now the law haunts me as a
cadaver haunts a living person. If I am not more than the law, then I am
among the damned souls the most damned.

For Nietzsche, son and grandson of Lutheran pastors a
century ago, that was natural enough. But what is Sartre up
to in insisting on the divine model? For he is very insistent
about it:[5]

When we speak of 'abandonment'—a favourite word of Heidegger—we
only mean to say that God does not exist, and that it is necessary to draw
the consequences of his absence right to the end. . . . The Existentialist . . .
finds it extremely embarrassing that God does not exist, for there dis-
appears with him all possibility of finding values in an intelligible heaven.
There can no longer be any good *a priori*, since there is no infinite and
perfect consciousness to think it. It is nowhere written that 'the good' exists,
that one must be honest or must not lie, since we are now upon the plane
where there are only men. Dostoevsky once wrote, 'If God did not exist,
everything would be permitted'; and that, for Existentialism, is the starting-
point.

Now why are atheists supposed to be so interested in this
God-shaped hole?

For Dostoevsky, of course, this concern is not surprising.
He was a real believer, a desperately unhappy man for whom
God alone gave meaning to the world. Removing God would,
therefore, have much the effect on him which it would for the
rest of us if the people we most loved died or betrayed us.
(Indeed the loss of faith often is felt as a betrayal *by* God; why
did he pretend to exist?) But if we suffer this blow, it is
certainly not because the people we loved have been the
'source of values' in the sense of inventing them, or establish-
ing them by all-powerful fiat or decree of the will, or showing
them to us in an 'intelligible heaven', or proving them *a priori*
—and are now shown to be mistaken. These vaguely Platonic
phrases do not represent at all the kind of thinking which goes
with our ordinary decisions whether things are good or bad.
Ordinarily we consult no authority, but look to see what *kinds*
of good and bad quality are present. And in bereavement we
suffer, because we know very well what we value, and we

found it in those we loved, but since they are gone it is no longer there, and a world without it is meaningless. As Othello says, when his suspicions against Desdemona have been lulled for the moment, 'when I love thee not, Chaos is come again'. Chaos comes when we lose those we love, not when we lose an omnipotent commanding authority. Commanding authorities, unloved, are no use as a source of value —a point on which we are all quite clear as soon as we remember the political context. Consider, too, what happens when Othello's suspicions are confirmed again. He cries out his farewell to the profession of arms, 'Othello's occupation's gone!' Now he did not value Desdemona as an infallible authority on strategy. This is the language of abandonment all right, but it is personal abandonment, personal love and loss. Nothing like this could follow from losing an infallible commanding authority. And certainly, if one really does not believe that the authority was ever there, it won't do to suggest that we are called upon to succeed him.

This is the step that I find really disreputable.

Terms like omnipotence, creation and the rest, unless they really do describe a divine being, are simply paranoid projections, delusions of grandeur, fantasies of 'infantile omnipotence'. Cultivation of these fantasies is not actually a sign of courage and realism (as Nietzsche supposed) but a piece of melodramatic exhibitionism. It means nothing. Nietzsche, of course, could overlook this point. He, in the 1870s, could still feel that blasphemy was *dangerous*; if he rang the bell and ran away, the lightning might still get him. At any rate he could count on upsetting the neighbours. But you don't ring the bell and run away at an empty house. And humanists are supposed by now to have got it into their heads that the house *is* empty. What humanism demands is surely that we speak of human beings as they are, not that we turn them into God-substitutes. Trying to do that twists our thoughts right away from reality. It perpetuates the worst, most irrational parts of religion without its saving graces. There is absolutely nothing to be said for self-worship.

Now what I have said so far may look rather crude to a religious believer. As I mentioned over Dostoevsky, however, I am not trying to deal at all with the believer's position, which is, if course, much more complicated. I am talking about the use of religious categories like creation by professed atheists like Nietzsche, Sartre and Heidegger, and particularly just now about Sartre's claim to be a humanist. I have suggested that you can't be 'abandoned' by something which never existed, still less by something which it would not make sense to suppose existing. If you discover that the being onto whom you projected your standards does not exist, it is your business to withdraw your projection. That is the adult response; inability to do so is childish. Your standards don't cease to be yours when you drop this piece of apparatus. The position seems much like that of someone who has put his faith in a political party, and discovers that the people running it are fools or knaves. If he has guts and understands the situation, he does not suppose himself deprived of his standards; he has simply got to think out for himself what his reasons were for adopting them in the first place.

Am I, however, being brutally unsympathetic? Does this talk of creation hold a serious point which I have missed?

Clearly, there are situations for which the strong language of creation does seem natural—points where there is a striking break and a new beginning in human life. Defending the creation language at this point, a more modest humanist might say this: Man made God in his own image; the myth of creating the world is merely a projection of something which actually happens when a human being has a new idea. *Man as God the Creator is not a paranoid fantasy; God is simply a projection of human originality.*

If we look at things this way, we must put the divine model, on which Sartre and Nietzsche lay so much stress, right aside. We must decide that their insistence on it is either just a piece of literary flamboyance, or a straight mistake. The proper model, the archetypal case of creation is, we shall now say, human originality. But this originality was the problem from which we started; analogies with God were meant to throw light on it. If they don't, it is going to have to be explained on its own terms. We must simply examine what we mean by it more carefully and closely. I find this idea much more promising. But how shall be proceed?

Now human originality certainly is a very mysterious thing.

The aspect of it which I think will help us most is one which almost does seem to call for the expression 'the world is always being created anew'. This is *individuality*, the simple difference that there naturally is between people. Your world isn't my world; the way in which we each see our public world is unique, unparalleled and irreplaceable. This, in fact, is one of the things meant by saying that 'each life is sacred', no duplicates are available. Chesterton put it well in discussing what makes the peculiar horror of suicide. He said that the murderer destroys just one man, but the suicide destroys the whole world—*his* world can never come again. And he knows it as the murderer does not know his victim's.

Now there is no doubt that this kind of individual difference has a great deal to do with actual innovations and inventions in thought. They are often made by people who, simply by nature, are peculiar, and are in the lucky position of being able naturally to make a move which is in a way obvious, and which their times call for, but which most people would not think of making. G. E. Moore seems to be an example of someone like this; Hobbes, Socrates, Rousseau, Dostoevsky and Blake might be others. Someone may be equipped to express an original and valuable idea merely by the fact that his character, and therefore his world, is by nature an extra-ordinary one. (Thus, the French call an eccentric person *un original*). *But* of course, individual creation in this sense doesn't depend on an act of the will. As Kant rightly said, genius is a part of nature, not an interruption or a supernatural intereference with the natural order; 'Genius is the innate mental aptitude *through which* nature gives the rule to art.'[6] Individuality of this sort is a natural asset which we can use or not, like our individual physique and temper. In a way, it's luck. We can't will it. It comes of our being the people that we are. Still, of course, nobody will be called *original* in the full, English sense of the word just for being unique; he has to do something original or 'creative'. What sort of thing will that be? Is this perhaps an act of the creative will?

Leaving art aside for the moment, if it is to lie in the field of ideals or values, there are two obvious possibilities. There is the public angle, the invention of a new institution or social form, and the private angle, the invention of a new way of looking at things. Good examples of the first might be Solon and Cleisthenes, the main architects of Athenian democracy, the people who worked out and set up in detail the first constitution in human history which made a serious and determined effort to give every citizen a real voice in government. Of the second, an instance might be Montaigne, with his remarkable moral courage, his lack of false modesty, his cheerful, unabashed curiosity about the self, about the workings of his own mind, which did so much to make modern psychology possible. But the two things, the outward institution and the inward way of thinking, must always go together to some extent. The new institution needs a new attitude of mind, and the new attitude must be translatable into action up to a point. Montaigne could hardly have thought like that if he had been a feudal serf of a Japanese Samurai. One swallow cannot possibly make a Renaissance.

I suggest these two examples because they do seem fairly striking innovations, and so come closer than most changes to meeting the demand for the sudden and totally unexpected which goes with the idea of creation. They are fairly big bangs. But this is only a matter of degree. The difficulty is still that *both are solutions to existing problems*, problems which had already to be felt as problems by numbers of people for the solution to be worked out, let alone accepted. And the importance of the solution depends on the public importance of the problem. No reformer, however original, can go far alone. His ideas are meant to apply to actual human life. If their application is not pretty frequently checked in discussion with others, they melt away back into private fantasy. And other people are not going to accept them without some reason.

Here we meet again the dilemma which, I have suggested, is so serious for Nietzsche and his followers. Are we talking about collective or individual projects? Collective ones, just because they are collective, must evolve, they can't be created by a sudden fiat. You can't be a reformer just by willing something to be good which previously was not so. Reformers have to work by showing their public that things *are* good which before did not seem so. They have to claim for their proposal advantages which already count as advantages, to solve problems which can already be seen to be problems. This is why words like *invent* or *discover* (which both mean find) are rightly more popular here than *create*. And *invent* is not normally used in the peculiar abstract sense in which Sartre talks of *inventing values*, but with reference to a given purpose. You can invent the spinning jenny, or a more humane form of divorce, or the notion of representative government, once you know that you want them. You can 'discover' the principle of religious toleration—but only, so to speak, if you are looking for it, if you already object to wars of religion. You can find an answer to a problem, even a new problem. The sense in which answers not yet found *exist* may be odd, but is really necessary. It is very strange to speak of *creating* an answer. Certainly everybody solving a hard problem needs a strong will. But that means that he needs sticking power, determination, resolution and independence. Will power alone doesn't generate answers. Nor can we make a bad answer into a good one simply by willing it to be so.

Yet of course it *is* true that a naturally original person does make a quite special contribution, because he sees the problem differently. How can we describe this?

How should we think about genius? Let us try a mining metaphor here. A peculiar man like Socrates or Blake is made, so to speak, of a different material from the rest of us. Inside him is a great vein of an extraordinary hard green stone, which he can mine to make statues and buildings. To say that what he produces depends on his will is to stress that he must do hard, practical, skilled work to do his mining. To speak of this will as *creative*, as essentially breaking with the past, may be just a way of pointing out that his stone is different from other people's, and makes different results possible. Or it may point to something much less interesting —to the fact that, in his mining, he must sometimes do things suddenly, with an explosion. In any case, it will only be a half-truth, because the stone itself, the original stuff of the personality is the essential thing. However hard the rest of us set our teeth and will, we cannot do just what Blake or Socrates does. No one else can come up with this particular hard, green stone.

Also, and especially in the case of artists, this image of

working a mine is often inadequate. Often they make us think more of a forest or lake, something which is extraordinary indeed, but which has *grown*. They may not break violently with the past at all; think of Shakespeare. And although most of them have to work hard too, they often stress that what they eventually produce seems much more found than deliberately carved—that it can astonish them and seem to come from outside. It is as if you dig your way into the mine, and *find* a statue. Michelangelo said that each block of stone has a statue inside it—the sculptor's job is only to chip away the surrounding stone. And many artists have spoken in this way of inspiration. This is what started all the talk of Muses. In such cases, it is very odd to make the will central.

Moreover, not every eccentric can (in the stronger, English sense) be called original or said to create. We call him so only if he can be followed. The buildings, once made, have to be ones that the rest of us can use and add to; the forest, once discovered, has to be one that the rest of us can enter. Originating is not just starting something; it is starting something worth going on with. An unusual person who cannot express himself easily must, unfortunately, leave us uncertain whether he is original or not. Often he partly succeeds in expressing himself; other people, who develop his suggestions, must then share the credit for what is created. Both in thought and in art, the most impressive achievements usually are collective ones. Socrates' work is developed by Plato, Aristotle and the others. Blake takes his place in the Romantic Movement. And what chiefly makes us call Blake original is not his most peculiar and unparalleled work, his Prophetic Books, but his painting and some of his poetry. The part, in fact, which it has proved possible for other people to follow.

All this is leading us away from the Big Bang notion of creation towards something much less dramatic and pretentious; and more like ordinary making. And of course, the word can be used much less pretentiously; with no Bang at all; it need not suggest Genesis. As I mentioned before, there are weaker senses. R. G. Collingwood discusses them well;

The word *create* is daily used in contexts that offer no valid ground for a fit of odium theologicum. . . . To create something means to make it nontechnically, but yet consciously and voluntarily. Originally, *create* means to generate, to make offspring, for which we still use its compound *procreate*. It is in this sense that we speak of creating a disturbance or a demand or a political system. The person who makes these things is acting voluntarily; he is acting responsibly; but he need not be acting in order to achieve any ulterior end. . , . It is in the same sense that Christians asserted, and Neo-Platonists denied, that God created the world.

Principles of Art, 128

This is supposed to destroy the mystery, to explain quite clearly how you can make something without knowing what you are making and still get credit for it, how you can have no ulterior end and yet achieve something important, which is not just a mistake. Does it succeed?

It may seem that at this point the word 'create' has been diluted into complete triviality, that it simply means 'make'. But it still keeps an awkward core of special meaning, and one that is important for Collingwood's theory of art. On his view, creators need not, indeed characteristically do not, know in advance what they are going to make. He sees the absence of a 'preconceived end' as a mark of real art, a mark which distinguishes it from mere craft. But if you really do not know what you are trying to bring about, it is hard to see how you can do it, and harder still to see how you can be called responsible. Artists don't in fact often talk in this way. They are often quite willing to discuss their aims and problems. But whether or not sense can be made of this for art, in morals it is surely a non-starter. Spontaneous feeling is an essential raw material for advances in morality, but it can't constitute them. Merely expressing it can't be the creation of values. Nor can merely acting in a new and unexpected way. People like Genghis Khan and or even Columbus don't create any values, though as a result of their activities new standards and values are no doubt often eventually called for. By contrast, people who act deliberately to bring about a preconceived end by setting up some new and valuable element in life do, like artists, make a distinctive contribution which has their own personal mark upon it. Collingwood's example of 'creating the English Navy' or a political system is of this kind, and it is quite different from those of creating a child or a disturbance, or international mistrust.

I suggest, therefore, that Collingwood's attempt to show a modest sense of creation which implies no preconceived purpose while still asserting responsibility won't work. It cannot therefore support his non-technical view of art. Nor—what is our present concern—can it support the idea of arbitrary and mindless creation in morals. If we want to understand how most reforms take place, we might do better to look at something which we would probably not describe as creation at all, though it does produce change, namely, personal example. This *can* alter standards, in fact, it is probably the central method of doing so. It is not glamorous and seldom receives medals—for instance, there must have been a lot of it about in the gradual development of mercy, as civilization unfolded:

> And some there be, which have no memorial;
> Who are perished as though they had never been.
> Their bodies are buried in peace
> But their name liveth for evermore.
> And these were merciful men. . . .
>
> (Ecclesiasticus 44. 9–10.)

This is just the kind of thing which in fact forms standards. And it is perfectly true that we would not talk of a *technique* of mercy. (Though, once the notion of mercy is there, techniques will gather round it—for instance, techniques of reconciliation and of turning away wrath.) It is true, too, that if there had been no such thing as mercy before, the first merciful man would have been an innovator of a quite dramatic kind, very much what we are looking for. But in fact, as animal comparisons show, mercy is, and has to be, an extremely ancient and gradual development, something *evolved* as a precondition of social life by any social species, not a sudden invention to transform it. And the same is true of the other virtues. Slow, painful evolution, not sudden cleverness nor divine fiat, puts them in our repertoire. This process does not particularly call for the name *creation*. It demands chiefly courage and clear-headedness. Innovators in this field innovate by their acts, not by new intellectual feats or by talk. Works of art are, I think, just a special class of such acts. Blake's or

Cézanne's works have their special signature on them—a peculiar combination of qualities, unknown before, but available later for imitation and development—in just the same way as the acts of Socrates or St Francis or Sir Thomas More. (All Works are Acts.) It is the combination that is new, not the elements. And that combination comes from a resolute working out of what each of these people had in them as their original character, not from an unaccountable sudden act of the creative will. Leaving gods out of the question, the source of creation does not lie in anybody's will. It lies (however simply and undramatically) in our inheritance, in the lives of our innumerable ancestors, and in the world which they have left us. It is they who gave us both our heredity and our culture. It is they who, through joys and ordeals inconceivable to us, forged that extraordinary thing, the human imagination:

> O, no man knows
> Through what wild centuries
> Roves back the rose. . . .
> (Walter de la Mare, 'All That's Past')

Only, of course, we take all that for granted.

4 G. E. MOORE ON THE IDEAL

G. E. Moore's *Principia Ethica* (1903) has had two distinct and rather confusing reputations. Professional philosophers have for the last fifty years treated it almost solely as the source of the notion that all reasoning in support of moral conclusions is vitiated by a 'naturalistic fallacy'. Moore's book, along with a rather grim article by H. H. Prichard called 'Does Moral Philosophy rest on a Mistake?'[1] was thought to establish this bizarre position, and so to prove that academic moral philosophers ought to keep out of all substantial moral argument, and occupy themselves only with 'meta-ethics', that is, with propounding and refining moral scepticism. Academics regarded it simply as a book about argument, and a negative, destructive one. This is hardly the stuff that fires enthusiasm and gives meaning to people's lives. But *Principia Ethica* did do that. It had a very wide sale and influence outside academic circles, primarily among people interested in the arts, to whom it had a quite different and entirely positive message. Clive Bell, whose lively book *Art* is largely an exposition and celebration of Moore's ideas, grows lyrical about it:

delicate and convincing piece of logic. . . . It is none of my business to do clumsily what Mr Moore has done exquisitely. I have no mind by attempting to reproduce his dialectic to incur the merited ridicule of those familiar with the *Principia Ethica* or to spoil the pleasure of those who will be wise enough to run out this very minute and order a masterpiece with which they happen to be unacquainted.

(*Art*, 1913, p. 80)

Are they talking about the same book? Yes, but different parts of it. The first five chapters do indeed make the negative case. But the sixth (called 'The Ideal') is as bold and positive a piece of substantial ethics as could be desired. For Moore,

though he thought it impossible to argue for one's moral
conclusions, still believed that they were matters of fact. He
was no emotivist. He thought that moral judgements were
either true or false, and that it was enormously important to
get the true ones. The reason why argument was irrelevant for
him was because you had only to look at the world to see what
was good. Prichard too thought like this, but when Prichard
looked at the world he saw right and wrong, and he saw them,
by a strange coincidence, exactly where they were placed by
the conventional thought of the day. Moore saw goodness,
and he saw it in quite unexpected places. With Prichard,
academic scepticism and defensiveness only reinforced moral
conservatism. Moore's position was much more interesting.
Moore actually did want to make a change in people's lives,
though it was a change in their way of thinking primarily,
rather than in their behaviour. He wanted to say that the real
centre of life, the thing that mattered most, was aesthetic
experience, 'the contemplation of beautiful objects'. Personal
relations were very important too, but their value sprang
chiefly from their being a cause or a setting for this experience. They consisted in the contemplation of other
people's physical beauty, and also of their mental qualities.
But:

Admirable mental qualities consist very largely in an emotional contemplation of beautiful objects; and hence the appreciation of them will
consist essentially in the contemplation of such contemplation. . . . Though,
therefore, we may admit that the appreciation of a person's attitude
towards other persons, or, to take one instance, the love of love, is far the
most valuable good we know, and far more valuable than the mere love of
beauty, yet we can only admit this if the first be understood to *include* the
latter, in various degrees of directness. . . .

Principia Ethica, p. 204

In this high praise, contemplation of natural beauty as well
as of art was included, and Moore in one place gave it a kind
of qualified priority (p. 195). But in general both his examples
and the term 'beautiful objects' which he constantly uses
suggest vases, symphonies and pictures rather than seas or
forests. His followers concentrated on art. If the doctrine had

been proposed today, the emphasis on nature would probably have been stronger, but it does not seem that Moore would have wanted to make it so.

With this emphasis, then, Moore's doctrine presents a bold and paradoxical development of the high valuation put on art by people like Wilde and Flaubert. Flaubert said, 'For an artist, there is only one thing; to sacrifice everything to art. He must regard life as a means, nothing else'. This leaves the artist as a rather mysterious exception among mankind. But suppose instead he were the type? Suppose he alone knows what life is really about? Stumping firmly ahead where Flaubert pointed, Moore reversed the move made by earlier philosophers from Plato on, who have asked, 'why have art?' and have answered by saying what good it did in terms of morality or religion. Not so, said Moore; nothing else has any intrinsic value, the question is, why have the rest of life? Morality itself is there only to make aesthetic experience possible:

It is only for the sake of these things [the contemplative pleasure of human intercourse and the enjoyment of beautiful objects] that anyone can be justified in performing any public or private duty; they are the *raison d'être* of virtue.

(p. 189)

Knowledge, freedom and justice have value only as means. And as for religion, the contemplation of beauty replaces it.

Moore was only 30 when *Principia Ethica*, came out, and it has the wildness of youth. It had immense influence on people concerned with the arts, who took its main point to lie in this last chapter. And Moore explicitly said that it did.

No one, probably, who has asked himself the question, has ever doubted that personal affection and the appreciation of what is beautiful in Art and Nature, are good in themselves, nor, if we consider strictly what things are worth having *purely for their own sakes*, does it appear probably that anyone will think that anything else has *nearly* so great a value. . . . This simple truth may, indeed, be said to be universally recognized. What has *not* been recognized is that it is the ultimate and fundamental truth of Moral Philosophy.

(p. 188–9)

Again on p. 27 he calls this 'the primary question' and 'the fundamental question of ethics' (p. 184). Philosophers have never known quite what to make of all this. They concentrated instead on the earlier, more destructive parts of the book, where Moore dismissed other people's ways of supporting morality (for instance by relating it to happiness). That is how chapters 1–5 came to be used alone as a sort of negative bible, a first blast of the trumpet against the use of argument in ethics. It was a sad and unsuitable fate for so vigorous and positive a book.

Moore's ideas on value deserve more attention. He brought contemplation of goodness and beauty back into the centre of the moral scene, where they had not stood since Plato. He balanced the busy over-emphasis on activity of the Protestant West by sounding a trumpet for the inner life. He gave a starting-point for answering Kant's emphasis on the will. Kant had said that nothing can be unconditionally good except the good will.[2] But can a will really be good without some receptiveness, some admiring contemplation of other good things? Plainly Moore has a point here. Totally unreceptive will would be blind and arrogant. But does the receptiveness have to be limited, as Moore limits it, to contemplation of beautiful objects? To many people it seems natural to let it expand into a faith in what lies behind beauty and speaks through it. Bell, who had no objection to metaphysics and did not at all mind casting ultimate reality for this role, thought this development into a true religion was right and inevitable (*Art* pp. 45–6). Maynard Keynes, who along with Bell, Lytton Strachey and Leonard Woolf was one of Moore's early disciples, says much the same thing:

> Our religion closely followed the English Puritan tradition of being chiefly concerned with the salvation of our own souls . . . I have called this faith a religion, and some sort of relation of Neo-Platonism it surely was. But we should have been very angry at the time with such a suggestion. We regarded all this as entirely scientific in character.
>
> ('My early beliefs', *Two Memoirs*, p. 86)

Keynes concluded that Moore's circle had a religion, but no morals, and that there were objections to this arrangement. Moore, however, was determined to be a consistent empiricist. This seemed to him to involve explaining the value of contemplation entirely in this-wordly terms, without using any religious concepts whatever. It is just this resolute humanism which makes his attempt so interesting.

Moore not only refused to appeal to any transcendent entity underlying beauty; he also refused to give beauty itself any special independent value, defining it firmly as 'that whereof the admiring contemplation is good'. This is puzzling. But whatever we may think of his solution, Moore's problem is a real one, not one of his own inventing. The view that art is, for some reason, enormously and perhaps overwhelmingly important, that it should in some way *take the place* of religion, is as widely held today as it was in 1903, and people's views on the reasons for this are still in extreme confusion. If Moore and Flaubert are heard, moral philosophy with all its problems would land in the lap of aesthetics. I do not think aestheticians have yet got news of this consignment of live snakes, loosely packed, moving in their direction.

To see what Moore himself meant to do with his idea, it is worth looking at his followers outside mainstream philosophy, notably his close friends, Keynes, Leonard Woolf, and (most revealing of all because least cautious) Clive Bell. All treat it as a creed you can live by, and indeed as the one they actually did live by. The only one with any real reservations is Keynes, and he arrived at them only after many years trial. In 1938, after thinking over the criticisms D. H. Lawrence had made many years before, he wrote the rather profound paper called 'My Early Beliefs'. Here he still declared his support of much that Moore had said, but added:

It is remarkable how wholly oblivious [Moore] managed to be of the qualities of the life of action and also of the pattern of life as a whole. . . . The New Testament is a handbook for politicians compared with the unworldliness of Moore's chapter on The Ideal. . . .

(pp. 93–4)

We repudiated all versions of the doctrine of Original Sin, of there being insane and irrational springs of wickedness in most men. We were not aware that civilization was a thin and precarious crust. . . . We had no respect for traditional wisdom or the restraints of custom. We lacked reverence, as Lawrence observed and as Ludwig [Wittgenstein] also used to say, for everything and everyone. It did not occur to us to respect the extraordinary accomplishment of our predecessors in the ordering of life (as it now seems to me to have been) or the elaborate framework which they had devised to protect this order.

(pp. 99–100)

(Compare Leonard Woolf, who resists this criticism, *Sowing* pp. 148–56.)

This is plainly right, and the damage extended even to the notion of art itself. Bell clearly thought he was following Moore in saying that the response to beauty must be thought-free as well as the response to goodness. Direct contemplation of a directly revealed value was required; any valuation involving thought was considered tainted. There must be no talk, for instance, of understanding the subject-matter or the artist's intentions:

The representative element in a work of art may or may not be harmful; always it is irrelevant. For, to appreciate a work of art, we need bring with us nothing from life, no knowledge of its ideas and affairs, no familiarity with its emotions. Art transports us from the world of man's activity to a world of aesthetic exaltation.

(*Art* p. 27)

Art is a religion. . . . Religion which is an affair of emotional conviction should have nothing to do with intellectual beliefs.

(ibid. pp. 181–3)

There is a muddle here which is natural but all the same disastrous. When something impresses us deeply, either in art or life, of course we do not necessarily know at once just what it is which is so good about it. We may long be baffled and unable to say at all what it is. We shall never be able to express it completely. And we must not dismiss this sort of vast and mysterious experience in favour of pronouncing on goodness and beauty by formula. But if mystery prevailed right across the board—if no articulation were *ever* possible— we should have no language for values at all. The point of having that language is that we want eventually to be able to talk about these things, to speak of them and hear about other people's insights, involving things which do *not* yet impress us—to be able to share our experiences with other people. Language makes this possible both for art and morals, though for morals it is much more obviously necessary. That is how literature works, it is also how criticism works. Without it Bell could hardly have developed and put about his theory that what made.things beautiful was significant form. (*Significant?* Of what?)

Thought matters. Contemplation, the unspeakable moment of insight, cannot, either in art or morals, enclose the whole of value for such a creature as man. It must lead to thought and action and they must flow directly from it, must be conceptually and not just causally linked to it. Good thought and action are attempts to express the ideal contemplated, in words and in life. It is a very odd thing about Moore's and Bell's exaltation of aesthetic experience that they treat it always as static and passive. Bell says little, and Moore nothing, about the *work* of the artist, which was a central theme with Flaubert and other art-exalters of the nineteenth century. And nobody mentions Aristotle's suggestion that contemplation is itself the most intense kind of activity, the hardest possible work.[3]

What distorted Moore's vision here was the pay-off pattern, otherwise known as moral consequentialism. This is the idea that only states really matter; only the results of action can have value. According to it, actions themselves and the people who do them are then not really good in themselves at all, but are only means to goodness. Freedom and knowledge, gas fires and the good will are all equally just useful, not actually good. This. view is a legacy from classical utilitarianism. Bentham, with characteristic simplicity, had been delighted to say that all conceivable value lay in the only possible pay-off, namely pleasure. Mill, a far subtler man, saw plenty of difficulties, but still tried to defend the position. He failed resoundingly, and at every turn his failures show the rightness of the insights which made him question the pay-off pattern, and the impossible crudeness, meanness, narrowness and arbitrariness which would be required to maintain it. Moore too saw the crudeness. But he thought it could be cured by merely changing the pay-off from pleasure to contemplation.

It may seem surprising that Moore, who was prepared to

criticize the utilitarians very sharply on other grounds, remained so dogmatic and undoubting in his insistence on consequentialism. Here we touch on the general problem of his dogmatism, the strange, rock-like character which made possible his extraordinary assumption that moral argument was unnecessary. Later, writing on other philosophical issues (as in his marvellous 'Defence of Common-Sense'),[4] Moore could be quite subtle and receptive to a variety of positions. But about ethics he showed a remarkable obtuseness to other people's insights. No doubt this was partly a matter of the epoch. Moore's and Prichard's unhistorical attitude was no accident. They ignored their predecessors' arguments, not because they were unconscious of change, but because they thought themselves part of one final change so tremendous that it put everything else out of date. They shared the belief, so common at the beginning of this century, that a single great change was happening to the world once and for all, which would make all previous art and thought irrelevant. (It is remarkable in how many spheres the name *modern* is still attached to something which began at that time.) They had no conception of adapting to continuous change. Besides this problem, it was Moore's personal weakness as well as his strength to be so massively simple, so single-minded in his own convictions that he sometimes found it almost impossible to grasp insights genuinely differing from his own. For all these reasons, he invariably treated Mill as a crude bungler. He exaggerated his own distinctiveness from him, and ignored the very obvious continuity. This waste of Mill's insights is specially disastrous at one of the many points where, even in *Utilitarianism*, Mill feels his way right past the pay-off pattern, and begins hesitantly to talk of virtue as an element in happiness rather than a means to it—language that he constantly used in *Liberty*. Moore sneers, as if this were not only a careless mistake but a piece of dishonesty, and hurries on.[5] He has reason to hurry. For Mill's move is necessary, and it damns consequentialism. Anyone who uses the means-end pattern has to help it out at some stage with the part-whole one. (Aristotle does it constantly.) You have then got to think out the relation between them. Mill certainly failed to do this. Moore could have tried to, but he preferred to cry 'heresy'.

Keynes says he used to make this very point that valuable wholes could extend through time, but could never get his friends to see it:

Indeed it is only states of mind that matter, provided we agree to take account of the pattern of life through time and give up regarding it as a series of independent, instantaneous flashes, but the ways in which states of mind can be valuable, and the objects of them, are more various, and also much richer, than we allowed for.

I fancy we used in old days to get round the rich variety of experience by expanding illegitimately the field of aesthetic appreciation (we would deal, for example, with all branches of the tragic emotion under this head), classifying as aesthetic experience what is really human experience, and somehow sterilizing it by this misclassification.

(*Two Memoirs*, p. 103)

But this compromise would have blown the whole scheme open, because once you allow states of mind to extend through time, you must think of them, not just as states, but as motives, which merge into actions. The abstraction which leaves out the actions themselves is crippling.

If only Moore had been taken seriously at once as the philosophic theorist of the aesthetic movement, these and many other fascinating points could have been argued. This would surely have led to some useful and important reasoning about the relation of art to religion and to life. It seems to me clear from the chapter on 'The Ideal' that in 1903 he did mean to be that theorist. Why was he not so understood? The answer, no doubt, lies in his style. Had Moore written like an angel, or even like Bertrand Russell, readers would probably not have overlooked his continuity with Baudelaire and Flaubert, Whistler and Wilde. Instead, vigorous though he is, he wrote with painful care, like an academic, indeed often like an old lawn-mower chugging over rough ground, arousing no suspicion of decadence. Here he was not alone. After the trial of Oscar Wilde, the light-heartedness went out of the aesthetic movement.[6] The painters whom Bell celebrated were not dandies like Degas and Whistler, but those deeply serious men, Cézanne and Van Gogh. Post-impressionism abstained entirely from peacock feathers and epigrams. But the style should not mislead us. The exaltation of art remained just as strong. Moore had by no means fully understood it, but he had extracted and expressed clearly one central element in it. If his reductive simplicy had been intelligently challenged, the many distinct reasons why art matters would have become much clearer, and its complex place in life could have been better understood.

5 TRYING OUT ONE'S NEW SWORD

All of us are, more or less, in trouble today about trying to understand cultures strange to us. We hear constantly of alien customs. We see changes in our lifetime which would have astonished our parents. I want to discuss here one very short way of dealing with this difficulty, a drastic way which many people now theoretically favour. It consists in simply denying that we can ever understand any culture except our own well enough to make judgements about it. Those who recommend this hold that the world is sharply divided into separate societies, sealed units, each with its own system of thought. They feel that the respect and tolerance due from one system to another forbids us ever to take up a critical position to any other culture. Moral judgement, they suggest, is a kind of coinage valid only in its country of origin.

I shall call this position 'moral isolationism'. I shall suggest that it is certainly not forced upon us, and indeed that it makes no sense at all. People usually take it up because they think it is a respectful attitude to other cultures. In fact, however, it is not respectful. Nobody can respect what is entirely unintelligible to them. To respect someone, we have to know enough about him to make a *favourable* judgement, however general and tentative. And we do understand people in other cultures to this extent. Otherwise a great mass of our most valuable thinking would be paralysed.

To show this, I shall take a remote example, because we shall probably find it easier to think calmly about it than we should with a contemporary one, such as female circumcision in Africa or the Chinese Cultural Revolution. The principles involved will still be the same. My example is this. There is, it seems, a verb in classical Japanese which means 'to try out one's new sword on a chance wayfarer'. (The word is *tsujigiri*, literally 'crossroads-cut'.) A samurai sword had to be tried out because, if it was to work properly, it had to slice through someone at a single blow, from the shoulder to the opposite flank. Otherwise, the warrior bungled his stroke. This could injure his honour, offend his ancestors, and even let down his emperor. So tests were needed, and wayfarers had to be expended. Any wayfarer would do—provided, of course, that he was not another Samurai. Scientists will recognize a familiar problem about the rights of experimental subjects.

Now when we hear of a custom like this, we may well reflect that we simply do not understand it; and therefore are not qualified to criticize it at all, because we are not members of that culture. But we are not members of any other culture either, except our own. So we extend the principle to cover all extraneous cultures, and we seem therefore to be moral isolationists. But this is, as we shall see, an impossible position. Let us ask what it would involve.

We must ask first: Does the isolating barrier work both ways? Are people in other cultures equally unable to criticize *us*? This question struck me sharply when I read a remark in *The Guardian* by an anthropologist about a South American Indian who had been taken into a Brazilian town for an operation, which saved his life. When he came back to his village, he made several highly critical remarks about the white Brazilians' way of life. They may very well have been justified. But the interesting point was that the anthropologist called these remarks 'a damning indictment of Western civilization'. Now the Indian had been in that town about two weeks. Was he in a position to deliver a damning indictment? Would we ourselves be qualified to deliver such an indictment on the Samurai, provided we could spend two weeks in ancient Japan? What do we really think about this?

My own impression is that we believe that outsiders can, in principle, deliver perfectly good indictments—only, it usually takes more than two weeks to make them damning. Understanding has degrees. It is not a slapdash yes-or-no matter. Intelligent outsiders can progress in it, and in some ways will be at an advantage over the locals. But if this is so, it must clearly apply to ourselves as much as anybody else.

Our next question is this: Does the isolating barrier between cultures block praise as well as blame? If I want to say that the Samurai culture has many virtues, or to praise the South American Indians, am I prevented from doing *that* by my outside status? Now, we certainly do need to praise other societies in this way. But it is hardly possible that we could praise them effectively if we could not, in principle, criticize them. Our praise would be worthless if it rested on no definite grounds, if it did not flow from some understanding. Certainly we may need to praise things which we do not *fully* understand. We say 'there's something very good here, but I can't quite make out what it is yet'. This happens when we want to learn from strangers. And we can learn from strangers. But to do this we have to distinguish between those strangers who are worth learning from and those who are not. Can we then judge which is which?

This brings us to our third question: What is involved in judging? Now plainly there is no question here of sitting on a bench in a red robe and sentencing people. Judging simply means forming an opinion, and expressing it if it is called for. Is there anything wrong about this? Naturally, we ought to avoid forming—and expressing—*crude* opinions, like that of a simple-minded missionary, who might dismiss the whole Samurai culture as entirely bad, because non-Christian. But this is a different objection. The trouble with crude opinions is that they are crude, whoever forms them, not that they are formed by the wrong people. Anthropologists, after all, are outsiders quite as much as missionaries. Moral isolationism forbids us to form *any* opinions on these matters. Its ground for doing so is that we don't understand them. But there is much that we don't understand in our own culture too. This brings us to our last question: If we can't judge other cultures, can we really judge our own? Our efforts to do so will be much damaged if we are really deprived of our opinions about other societies, because these provide the range of comparison, the spectrum of alternatives against which we set what we want to understand. We would have to stop using the mirror which anthropology so helpfully holds up to us.

In short, moral isolationism would lay down a general ban on moral reasoning. Essentially, this is the programme of immoralism, and it carries a distressing logical difficulty. Immoralists like Nietzsche are actually just a rather specialized sect of moralists. They can no more afford to put moralizing out of business than smugglers can afford to abolish customs regulations. The power of moral judgement is, in fact, not a luxury, not a perverse indulgence of the self-righteous. It is a necessity. When we judge something to be bad or good, better or worse than something else, we are taking it as an example to aim at or avoid. Without opinions of this sort, we would have no framework of comparison for our own policy, no chance of profiting by other people's insights or mistakes. In this vacuum, we could form no judgements on our own actions.

Now it would be odd if Homo sapiens had really got himself into a position as bad as this—a position where his main evolutionary asset, his brain, was so little use to him. None of us is going to accept this sceptical diagnosis. We cannot do so, because our involvement in moral isolationism does not flow from apathy, but from a rather acute concern about human hypocrisy and other forms of wickedness. But we polarize that concern around a few selected moral truths. We are rightly angry with those who despise, oppress or steamroll other cultures. We think that doing these things is actually *wrong*. But this is itself a moral judgement. We could not condemn oppression and insolence if we thought that all our condemnations were just a trivial local quirk of our own culture. We could still less do it if we tried to stop judging altogether.

Real moral scepticism, in fact, could lead only to inaction, to our losing all interest in moral questions, most of all in those which concern other societies. When we discuss these things, it becomes instantly clear how far we are from doing this. Suppose, for instance, that I criticize the bisecting Samurai, that I say his behaviour is brutal. What will usually happen next is that someone will protest, will say that I have no right to make criticisms like that of another culture. But it is most unlikely that he will use this move to end the discussion of the subject. Instead, he will justify the Samurai. He will try to fill in the background, to make me understand the custom, by explaining the exalted ideals of discipline and devotion which produced it. He will probably talk of the lower value which the ancient Japanese placed on individual life generally. He may well suggest that this is a healthier attitude than our own obsession with security. He may add, too, that the wayfarers did not seriously mind being bisected, that in principle they accepted the whole arrangement.

Now an objector who talks like this is implying that it *is* possible to understand alien customs. That is just what he is trying to make me do. And he implies, too, that if I do succeed in understanding them, I shall do something better than giving up judging them. He expects me to change my present judgement to a truer one—namely, one that is favourable. And the standards I must use to do this cannot just be Samurai standards. They have to be ones current in my own culture. Ideals like discipline and devotion will not move anybody unless he himself accepts them. As it happens, neither discipline nor devotion is very popular in the West at present. Anyone who appeals to them may well have to do some more arguing to make *them* acceptable, before he can use them to explain the Samurai. But if he does succeed here, he will have persuaded us, not just that there was something to be said for them in ancient Japan, but that there would be here as well.

Isolating barriers simply cannot arise here. If we accept something as a serious moral truth about one culture, we can't refuse to apply it—in however different an outward form—to other cultures as well, wherever circumstance admit it. If we refuse to do this, we just are not taking the other culture seriously. This becomes clear if we look at the last argument used by my objector—that of justification by consent of the victim. It is suggested that sudden bisection is quite in order, *provided* that it takes place between consenting adults. I cannot now discuss how conclusive this justification is. What I am pointing out is simply that it can only work if we believe that *consent* can make such a transaction respectable—and this is a thoroughly modern and Western idea. It would probably never occur to a Samurai; if it did, it would surprise him very much. It is *our* standard. In applying it, too, we are likely to make another typically Western demand. We shall ask for good factual evidence that the wayfarers actually do have this rather surprising taste—that they are really willing to be bisected. In applying Western standards in this way, we are not being confused or irrelevant. We are asking the questions which arise *from where we stand*, questions which we can see the sense of. We do this because asking questions which you can't see the sense of is humbug. Certainly we can extend our questioning by imaginative effort. We can come to understand other societies better. By doing so, we may make their questions our own, or we may see that they are really forms of the questions which we are asking already. This is not impossible. It is just very hard work. The obstacles which often prevent it are simply those of ordinary ignorance, laziness and prejudice.

If there were really an isolating barrier, of course, our own culture could never have been formed. It is no sealed box, but a fertile jungle of different influences—Greek, Jewish, Roman, Norse, Celtic and so forth, into which further influences are still pouring—American, Indian, Japanese, Jamaican, you name it. The moral isolationist's picture of separate, un-mixable cultures is quite unreal. People who talk about British history usually stress the value of this fertilizing mix, no doubt rightly. But this is not just an odd fact about Britain. Except for the very smallest and most remote, all cultures are formed out of many streams. All have the problem of digest-ing and assimilating things which, at the start, they do not understand. All have the choice of learning something from this challenge, or, alternatively, of refusing to learn, and fighting it mindlessly instead.

This universal predicament has been obscured by the fact that anthropologists used to concentrate largely on very small and remote cultures, which did not seem to have this problem. These tiny societies, which had often forgotten their own history, made neat, self-contained subjects for study. No doubt it was valuable to emphasize their remoteness, their extreme strangeness, their independence of our cultural tradition. This emphasis was, I think, the root of moral isolationism. But, as the tribal studies themselves showed, even there the anthro-pologists were able to interpret what they saw and make judgements—often favourable—about the tribesmen. And the tribesmen, too, were quite equal to making judgements about the anthropologists—and about the tourists and Coca-Cola salesmen who followed them. Both sets of judgements, no doubt, were somewhat hasty, both have been refined in the light of further experience. A similar transaction between us and the Samurai might take even longer. But that is no reason at all for deeming it impossible. Morally as well as physically, there is only one world, and we all have to live in it.

6 THE OBJECTION TO SYSTEMATIC HUMBUG

Is it quite all right to shake hands with murder in your heart?

I   The Nature of the Problem

The view that our feelings don't concern morality, that we have no duties about them, that it does not matter how we feel so long as we act correctly, is often attributed to Kant. As we shall see, this is an mistake. But it is not surprising that people have credited Kant with such a view. He did lay himself open to that suspicion, because he was too busy shooting at contrary errors to resist it.

It *is* surprising, however, that this view has, seriously and unmistakably, been put forward and prevailed in the central British empiricist tradition. I call this surprising, because one might hope that empiricists would be more careful than rationalists over questions about feeling. G. E. Moore ruled that our feelings were outside our control *almost always*. (He didn't discuss the rare exceptions, and his followers have paid no attention to them, so I shall ignore them here.) We can normally control nothing but our outward actions, he said, so our normal duties can only require these actions. So precepts like 'love your neighbour' or 'thou shalt not covet' cannot possibly be understood literally and seriously as commands meant to be carried out. He concludes that they are just hypothetical commands, saying what *would* have been our duty if we had been able to do it.[1]

This is odd. Why should such hypothetical commands concern us at all—any more than, say, the instructions in a book on athletic training concern the paraplegic who leafs through it for amusement? Moore did not explain. Like Mill, no doubt, he simply took it for granted that a sharp line divided all judgments about action logically from judgments about any sort of motive, including feeling. 'The motive has nothing to do with the morality of the action, though much with the worth of the agent.'[2] For he too, like Mill, believed that the rightness or wrongness of actions was entirely a matter of their consequences. And he was just as bankrupt as Mill was, and as any other consequentialist must be, on the question what 'the worth of the agent' might mean.[3]

Since Moore, British empiricists have paid even less attention to the topic, which withered in the brief but arid summer of dogmatic behaviourism. Mill's idea that feeling was irrelevant to morality, and Moore's that it was un-controllable, no doubt prepared people's minds to accept the suggestion that it was more or less non-existent. They expressed this usually in the easiest possible way, namely by ignoring it. Interesting arguments to support the position can however be found, e.g. in Stuart Hampshire's *Thought and Action*.

That inner feeling is altogether 'mythical' or non-existent is a peculiar metaphysical position, which belongs to crude, primitive Watsonian behaviourism. Philosophers usually avoid it because it is so mysterious; what could it mean to say that what evidently occurs, and is part of experience, is unreal? (That rather crude instrument, Occam's Razor, cannot deal with such questions.) The point of more subtle forms of behaviourism, however, is to suggest that, though real enough, inner feeling is, for this or that purpose, *un-important*. Philosophers as well as psychologists have often had occasion to say this. But the purposes for which they think it unimportant vary, and so do the more important things which they want to bring forward in its place. Since im-portance is entirely relative to purpose, this means that their doctrines are very different, and need to be argued separately. (Compare the position of someone who said, quite generally, that 'plants are unimportant'. Without a context, this is nonsense.) It is an interesting and unlucky fact that the words in which such views are naturally put tend to approximate them to each other, and to the simple metaphysical doctrine of non-existence. (People still reach for Occam's Razor, however little it helps them.) In ordinary thought, the ideas of

unreality and unimportance are very closely linked. Dreams,
phantoms and pink rats are called unreal, not because they
don't occur, but because they don't matter. That is why
unsophisticated people, reading *The Concept of Mind*, commonly take Ryle to be saying that mind is unreal, simply
because he constantly plays down the importance of inner
factors, not just in relation to this or that purpose, but
generally.

In *Thought and Action* (which is a far more subtle book)
Hampshire makes great efforts to avoid this wholesaleness.
He carefully concedes that inner struggles and the like are not
mythical or illusory. In fact he stresses their importance *as
preludes to action*, and declares the wholeness of morality
against those who want to reduce it to talk:

The 'reduction' of moral judgements to quasi-orders and recommendations
is like the behaviourist's reduction of inner thoughts and feelings to their
natural expression in behaviour; it is a confusion between necessary precondition and the essential nature of that which develops from it.

(p. 143)

But in spite of this he insists that nothing that goes on within
is to count literally as an action. 'Mental actions', even if so
described, are not *real actions*. (Compare 'real coffee' or 'real
cream'.) They have only a 'shadowy and parasitical nature'.
They depend for full realization on their being later translated
into outward form (p. 163). In them there is 'no performance'
(p. 160) nothing which we try to do and can succeed or fail in
doing. They are not part of 'the only solid and substantial
world that there is' (p. 163).

What does this mean? If we are not doing ontology, the
most natural interpretation seems to be the moral one, which
says that what we think and feel has little or no importance or
value unless it produces outward action, that we ought not to
be much interested in it. It is worth noting that *Moore* could
never have endorsed this view, since he said firmly that 'by far
the most valuable things which we know or can imagine, are
certain states of consciousness' (*Principia Ethica* p. 188). In
Hampshire's view, however, conscious states cannot be

assessed or valued apart from the action they produce, and this not just because of the ignorance of the bystander, but from the subject's own angle as well. We need a moral argument for this. We need to compare the merits, the value, of concentrating on one's inner life with those of concentrating on one's outer, to look at excesses at both extremes, and to show where the right balance lies. But to do this would absolutely require us to admit the reality of the inner life. If we are to blame the introverted and the contemplative, we must blame them for what they actually do. This cannot be reduced to their *failure* to act outwardly. There could be all sorts of reasons for that, and introversion is only one of them.

It cannot be right, either, to suggest as Hampshire does that thoughts and feelings which do not lead to action are unimportant because, though real, they are actually rather *rare*, a somewhat perverse and artificial occasional product of over-civilization:

A man to whom we attribute a rich inner life of belief and disbelief, of unexpressed doubt and self-questioning, must be a man of great powers of self-restraint, to whom the inhibition of action is natural. He has cut away the substance of human routines and chosen to live with their shadow. He does not shout, but he exults inwardly. . . . This habit of inhibition, which replaces the substance of perceptible behaviour with its shadow in the mental life of thought and feeling, is the process of civilization.

(p. 165)

This is an empirical remark, and it is contrary to experience. Throughout human life, thought constantly exceeds action, not because action is suppressed, but because the imagination is so rich and fertile. It constantly produces twenty times as much material as could possibly be lived, much of it of a kind which could not possibly point that way. Keats's sonnet:

> When I have fears that I may cease to be
> Before my pen hath gleaned my teeming brain,

rightly speaks of *teeming*. The difference between him and the rest of us is not the quantity of the harvest, but in the quality.

Obvious further examples are the wide speculative curiosity of young children—particularly their love of stories—and the strong continuing fascination of gossip, even about people we shall never meet. These things are obviously among the roots of art. It is true that in the long run we do manage to use much of this stuff for action, and that we think we should try to do so. But—as is notorious in the case of scientific research—we cannot tell in advance which parts will be usable. We do not collect it for use, but for delight and because we cannot possibly help it. If this did not happen, art would be quite inexplicable. Hampshire, unlike Ryle, minds about making sense of art, and it causes him bad headaches. He has to treat it as something exceptional and paradoxical, an occasional white blackbird, a centre of peculiar mental activities which mysteriously *do* have value even though they do not lead to action.[4] In general, he rules, 'thought cannot be thought, as opposed to day-dreaming or musing, unless it is directed towards a conclusion, whether in action or judgement' (p. 159). So what is wrong with day-dreaming or musing? After all, they are normally included as ways of 'thinking'. Day-dreaming may perhaps be treated as by definition idle, but *musing* is quite general. It would naturally cover all Keats's reflections in the sonnet just mentioned, notably those he concludes with:

> Then on the shore
> Of the wide world I stand alone, and think,
> Till love and fame to nothingness do sink.

and Shakespeare's:

> When in disgrace with fortune and men's eyes
> I all along beweep my outcast state—
>
> (Sonnet 29)

and,

> When to the sessions of sweet silent thought
> I summon up remembrance of things past—
>
> (Sonnet 30)

Here they are describing what they do. And what they do is certainly not just preparing to write poetry. Nor, of course, is it just weeping, moaning etc. and preparing to do more of that. Expressive acts can be performed by *actors*. They do not give point to feelings, but vice versa.

The dismissal of day-dreaming and musing has, I think, to be a moral judgement, a remark about the part such things should properly play in life.

Hampshire, however, does not pursue this moral enquiry. Instead, he uses decidedly ontological language. What is *shadowiness*? Hampshire defends talk of shadows as an 'almost unavoidable metaphor' (p. 160). But it seems quite unsuitable. The relation between a shadow and the tree that casts it is almost opposite to that between murderous thoughts and the murder they point to. First, the causal direction had been reversed. Trees cause shadows; possible future events cannot cause present thoughts, but vice versa. Second, the direction of representation is also wrong, though this is perhaps a little less obvious. Murderous thoughts are not photographic copies or reflections cast by that unavailable event, a future murder: after all, it may never occur. They are projections of existing motives, which indeed they *represent*, though in a subtler sense—they express them, they body them forth. Those motives, along with existing information, determine all details of the plan. They are thoughts: such thoughts are as real as TNT. They can be quite as influential. But their reality does not consist in, or depend on their being so. Both thoughts and TNT exist fully and have their own properties. They can be studied in themselves, not only in their actual or likely effects.

I cannot here go into these ontological questions properly. I think myself that 'the only substantial and solid world that there is' must contain people's thoughts and feelings along with all its other jumble of real features. I believe Hampshire thinks this too. There is no need for special kinds or degrees of reality. Nor can things depend for their reality on their actual or likely effects. They can, however, depend for their *value* on these. Some things do. Toothbrushes and teaspoons, for instance, have value only as means. The question is, are human thoughts and feelings in the same position? This question cannot be decided by branding them as having an inferior kind of reality. Ontologically, there are no second-class citizens.

If I am right in turning from the ontological to the moral question, what Hampshire is doing is telling us not to be content with thoughts and feelings as substitutes for outer acts. He is insisting, as behaviourists too have rightly done, on the importance of outer activity, and therefore on the unsatisfactoriness of idealist models (including Hume's) which show it as a shadowy by-product of thought. He is making room for such moral points as Sartre expresses more directly—that it is no use claiming to be a worker unless you work, a writer unless you write, or a lover unless you do something about it. 'There is no love apart from the deeds of love.'[5] Both Moore and Mill were no doubt also interested in this same theme. It is a moral point of obvious importance, something which really needs saying to idealists and to moralists absorbed in the extremer versions of justification by faith. But it is still one-sided. Exclusive attention to it leads to moral results every bit as repulsive, eccentric and pointless as the contrary obsession.

II   The Moral Issue

To show this, I shall illustrate now what is wrong with Moore's moral position by an example. I take, out of a great range, a rather simple and schematic one which I hope will fit a wide variety of situations, primitive and civilized, private and public, academic and political.

Example   Peter and George, once friends, have long been carrying on a feud. It had a point once, and those concerned have much enjoyed it. But it is now growing clearly pernicious to their parties and even to themselves. They see that they must unite against a common threat. So a reconciliation is arranged. They see the need for this and accept it fully, and tomorrow they are to meet to confirm it publicly. So what do they do today?

Peter does what I suggest most of us would try to do in his

situation. While carrying on his ordinary outward occupations, he tries to do something about the tumult which the
prospect produces in his feelings. He tries, however feebly,
confusedly, and unwillingly, to get into a more possible frame
of mind for this difficult meeting. He makes an effort to think
about George in a way foreign to his recent habits—not as a
type-cast enemy, but as an individual with his own feelings,
an individual whom he once knew. He tries to check his
habitual spiteful brooding on George's sins, and to remind
himself for once of the provocations which he himself has
given. Spasms of shame for once get a hearing. And so on. It
doesn't work well, he has an upsetting afternoon—but still,
he tries.

But George, who has been reading Moore, does nothing of
the sort. His feelings, he sees, are in no way under his
control. He pays them no attention; they continue to seethe as
usual, but he knows that he must behave correctly and make a
friendly impression. For this he relies on what is significantly
called *acting*. So he spends the afternoon practising friendly
gestures in the glass, and the evening briefing his aides on
how they should smile, where they should stand, what
remarks they should feed him. . . .

Peter, in fact, tries to alter his feelings to fit the acts he
knows he ought to do. George ignores his feelings entirely and
concentrates on getting the act exactly right. Common sense
has several points to make about the contrast:

1 *Both enterprises are possible.* It is simply a mistake to
assume, as Moore did, that what Peter attempts can't be
done. Certainly it can't be done *completely*. Certainly it is hard,
and more in the nature of an endless project that one takes on
than a smartly completable 'duty' as featured on the duty-
sergeant's list. But then, very many duties are of this kind—
for instance, the duty to help somebody, or mankind's duty to
put an end to war, which Kant discussed so shrewdly in his
book *Perpetual Peace*. To say that we can't complete a job is
never to say that we can do nothing about it.

Moreover, George's project, too, has exactly the same
drawback. He needs to take people in; can he do that *completely*?
He may set himself a moderate pass standard, such as not

waking obvious suspicion—but then Peter too can set himself a pass standard if he likes. Beyond that, a vista stretches before George of *degrees* of cordiality which he might register, degrees of confidence which he might evoke—the actor's life is not really very like the duty-sergeant's. Prolonged acting, continued off the stage and quite unsupported by feeling, is not only exhausting, it is interminable. This brings us to the second point:

2 *Normally, both things will be attempted, and attempted as aspects of a single project.*   One enterprise will simply not make sense without the other. (Peter, too, must pay some attention to outward preparations, though they will be different ones.) The division of act and motive is, in the great range of normal cases, a vicious abstraction, and the motive must include the feeling. And this is still true although:

3 *There does exist a range of cases where, for special reasons, we distinguish and contrast them.*   There are some outward duties which really can be performed effectively even without bringing oneself to a suitable state of feeling—for instance, sending money through the post, or performing simple manual work while nobody else is present. This kind of case seems to have obsessed moralists like Moore, Sartre and Hampshire. They are struck by the hypocrisy of those who support their refusal to wash up, by claiming, *either* that they are offering feeling instead, *or* that suitable feeling is absent, and that this makes the action impossible. To hypocrites of this kind, it is right to say that 'there is no love apart from the deeds of love'. This corrective, however, seems most often called for in public and political life, which is the chief domain of empty feeling. Private, personal life, by contrast, seems rather more often prone to the contrary plague of hypocrisy by empty *acts*, dead ritual or emotional exploitation. 'She lives for others; you can tell the others by their hunted look.' In dealing with people whom you actually meet, you have got to have more of love than the deeds. Still further, and more startlingly:

4 *There also exists a range of cases, and pretty important ones, where all that matters is the feeling*. It makes perfectly good sense that

we should be ashamed of some feelings, regardless of likely consequences:

> Remembering that night long afterwards, Ivan recalled with particular disgust how he would suddenly get up from the sofa and quietly, as though terribly afraid to be seen, open the door, go out on the landing and listen to his father moving about and walking in the rooms on the floor below—he had listened for a long time, for about five minutes, with a sort of strange curiosity, with bated breath and a thumping heart. But why he had done all this, why he was listening, he did not of course know himself. That 'action' of his he called 'contemptible' all his life afterwards; and deep inside him, in the recesses of his heart, he thought of it as the vilest action of all his life.
>
> (*The Brothers Karamazov*, Part II, Book 5, Ch. 7)

The reasons for Ivan's view are good enough and I do not want to over-simplify them here. Putting it baldly, I suppose the point is that in those moments he positively gave up trying to make sense of the confusion surrounding his father and resist the gathering evil. He dropped instead into the role of a passive and voyeuristic spectator—observing, as at a play, the old man's lustful and anxious waiting for Grushenka; consenting, as at a play, that the next act should, if it so chanced, reveal that his despised step-brother will murder the old man, making no change in his decision to leave early in the morning, endorsing, by his passiveness, the intentions of that step-brother whom he loathes, becoming his puppet. He gave up. On 'behaviourist' views, the only thing wrong with that is that it makes his father's murder more likely. But it follows from this that everything would be quite all right if he could keep this state of mind and merely *act* differently. Or again, that if his actions were fixed and he must in any case leave in the morning, it would not matter what he felt. In fact, more generally, it would never matter how abysmally mean and odious our motives were, provided it could be guaranteed that we were also too cowardly and apathetic ever to act on them. Feelings, on this view, have value only as a means, like a sum of money or a piece of furniture. And this is psychological nonsense. I say this flatly; I shall be expanding the point. But it brings me to the most interesting side of the matter— namely, why systematic humbug, however skilful, won't do;

why we can't accept George's methods, even if they were
made completely and lastingly effective.

What consideration moves us to reject that bargain? A
number of names could be given to it—common honesty,
straightforwardness, sincerity, simple-mindedness, even a
kind of laziness, but a very special kind. Actually, many
people in this position, if they were asked why they did *not*
take up systematic humbug, and offered a course in perfecting
it, would hardly know what to answer, so obvious, so central
and taken for granted is the objection. 'I couldn't live like
that'—but why not? The objection is in fact the missing piece
of many puzzles, a piece too little noticed by empiricists, one
which makes nonsense of any sharp division between action,
thought and feeling. It is our need for coherence—for the
unity of the personality. We cannot accept a radical, lasting
separation between our inner and our outer lives without
mortal damage. The continuity between them is not just
contingent and associative; it is conceptual. Dislocate the
logic of the emotions, and life becomes, not just unfamiliar, but
deeply unintelligible and inhuman. We all fear madness. In
spite of recent romanticizations of it, each of us still endorses
this fear as completely justified. And it is a fear of that
dislocation. The active core of the personality will not have
disruption of this kind. Man is not held together only by
consistent thought or by the shape of the surrounding land-
scape. He holds himself together (up to a point and with great
difficulty) by virtue of a *feeling*—a strong wish for order and
unity.

III   What Practical Reason Is

But this wish, this feeling, this motive, has in common speech
a very interesting name. It is called Reason. Making sense of
one's life is what 'reason demands'.[6] Going to pieces is 'losing
one's reason'. And Peter will naturally think of his enterprise
as an attempt to 'reason with himself', to be more rational
and reasonable. Now this cannot just mean 'consistent in his
thoughts'. Mere intellectual consistency is compatible with all
sorts of aims; you have only to drop those which turn out not

to fit in. There is nothing internally inconsistent about George's project, provided he chooses his premisses. The maxim that 'one should always deceive others when convenient' would fit quite well, for instance, in a framework of strict Hobbesian egoism, or of a carefully Benthamite utilitarianism; better still into one of solipsism. That doesn't settle the question whether these views are themselves rational or reasonable. Here we want more than internal consistency. We ask, are they frameworks suitable to contain the aims of such a creature as man? Or, of course, of whatever other species a rational being may belong to. Actually, even to test their consistency, we would have to consider the conditions of life for that species, and among those conditions is a given emotional constitution. So we have to consider general type of feeling, as well as thoughts and actions.

When Peter struggles against his vindictiveness as an 'unreasonable feeling' he means by this that it does not make sense in the context of other feelings necessary and proper to human beings. And if, on the other hand, he gives way to it, thereby involving everybody in ruin, he is guilty of an *irrational* vindictiveness—that is, one for which no serious human aim provides a justification, one which is slightly mad. This would still hold even if he had managed to evolve an internally consistent Luciferian system of topsy-turvy aims to justify it, unless that system itself had somehow been meshed convincingly into the framework of human needs. No one has yet shown signs of succeeding in doing this, although immoralists have long been promising it.[7] In fact, it may well be time to prosecute immoralism for fraud under the Trades Descriptions Act.

This is how the notions of reasonableness and rationality work. And that is why Hume went wrong in his discussion of what is unreasonable. He viewed 'reason' simply as a fact-finding capacity. He therefore said; 'It is not contrary to reason for me to prefer the destruction of the whole world to the scratching of my finger' (*Treatise*, Book II, Part III, Section 3). But anyone in a position to say 'me' and 'my finger' must be a member of a given primate species, with a given repertory of satisfactions. He is also, since he uses language, a member of a given culture, and one who recognizes others as present for him to speak to—therefore no solipsist. If he can *prefer*, he is a being already mature enough to compare prospects, one who has therefore already narrowed down the given repertoire to form a system of priorities. He is not a blank, disembodied intellect. His next job is to think what the new proposal means, what it involves, what follows from it, to what it commits him, how it affects his existing aims. He tries to understand what principles of choice could go with it or dictate it. We call proposals *unreasonable* when we cannot get intelligible answers to these questions, or when those suggested would not fit in with other necessary elements of human life in any way that makes sense.

When we tackle these points, our reflection has all the obvious marks of reasoning. It can be consistent or inconsistent, clear or confused, relevant or irrelevant, a solution or a failure. And on all these points other people, if properly informed, can judge as well as ourselves. But it is *practical* reasoning. So Hume doesn't recognize it.

His mistake is even more instructively clear on the previous page where he calls Reason the Slave of the Passions. He does this in well-justified protest against the misleading picture of a *conflict* between Passion and Reason. But his employment model is no better. *All* dramatizations which set 'Reason' as one participant over against other aspects of the personality are confused. We are still suffering from the Romantic Revival's insistence on doing this, with the hope of making Reason somehow the villain of the piece, when in fact it is more like the containing scene of the drama. All such dramatizations, including Hume's, make the real continuity of our nature inexpressible.

To show this we must ask how, on Hume's model, 'the passions' would ever reach agreement on the orders to be passed to Reason. Outside the committee-room door sits speculative Reason, the slave or secretary. It has provided the factual data, and is waiting to be told what to do. Inside are the Passions, arguing. Vindictiveness, vanity, ambition, laziness and the rest shout louder and louder; how are they to agree? Such a secretary, unless it does what secretaries sometimes do and decides for itself what to put in the minutes, will have nothing to act on. What has gone wrong? Simply that, by Reason, we do not mean such an inactive secretary, but at least the Chairman, and more plausibly the whole well-ordered gathering. We mean the core of the personality, the central I, the subject who owns 'the passions' as his attributes, who is himself vindictive, vain and all the rest of it, but who is more than these attributes, and can, unless he abdicates, to some extent arbitrate between them, and decide gradually which sort of person to be. He—that subject— feels, thinks *and* acts. The relation between these aspects of his life is never just contingent. They must all be seen as expressions of a single personality. In that context, it is sharply evident that some arrangements make better sense than others, and many make no sense at all. The question how we distinguish them, and what are the problems of doing so, is one of enormous practical and theoretical importance. It is one on which the tradition of Mill and Moore is systematically bankrupt, though (as for instance Butler or William James can show) such bankruptcy is not at all necessary to empiricism.

If we want serious and realistic philosophic discussion of choice, of the various ways in which our central self finds expression, we must turn to the tradition of Kant. It is not anti-empiricist to do this. An empiricist is, basically, a fellow who wants the facts considered, who respects the complexity of experience and will not sacrifice it to a slick intellectual scheme. But experience shows us that:

1. in general, the human personality is really very complex, and
2. in particular, one of the most striking facts about it is its need for unity, for an order that will make that complexity manageable.

Each of us has only one life to live, and needs therefore to live it as some sort of coherent whole. Emphasis on this can be called rationalism. But if so, it is of a kind which is in no way opposed to empiricism, but completes it, since it is needed for the proper describing of experience. And the slick intellectual scheme proposed by Moore gives us the worst of both worlds.

Its attempts to be economical make it downright cheap and shoddy. It misrepresents experience entirely.

IV Kant's View

What, then, about Kant?

Kant said that act and motive must be seen as continuous and judged as a whole. He called this whole the will. His main purpose was to show that the will was the proper seat of value—that nothing except the good will can be always and unconditionally good.[8] In particular, he wanted to say that neither happiness nor any kind of feeling can have this supreme, unconditional, all-weather value. He makes it clear that the will is not just idle good intention, such as paves the road to hell, but 'the straining of every means so far as they are in our power' (p. 60). This avoids the vicious abstraction of act from motive. And he also insists that the good will is a rational will, avoiding the abstraction of choice from thought. Altogether, he takes so much trouble to make the will comprehensive that the right criticism of him might be, not that he has picked the wrong component of the self as the true subject of praise, but that what he has picked is the responsible self as a whole, and not any one of its components. This may, I think, be what makes his exaltation of the will look so attractive. And it may well be the best way to develop his insight, the right resolution of the clash between will and feeling. But Kant, because he was opposing people who exalted feeling absurdly, saw this clash as irresoluble. He weighed feeling against will and said that, though feeling does have value, its value is inferior and conditional on the presence of a good will. We may perhaps do better to say, in the end, that it has a different kind of value, both kinds being necessary to the whole and not in competition. But we must certainly also say that these two kinds of value are intelligibly related.

Kant treats feeling as something accidental, contingent. But it is not contingent. Feelings are not bare matter, bare sensation. They have their form, the thought which they enshrine, and the form always limits the possible matter.

Curiosity cannot *feel* like a longing for ice cream, nor vindictiveness like wanting a day in the country. And these are necessary, not contingent truths.

This is Kant's trouble. His empiricist critics have never taken it seriously enough. They could not do so, because they too were committed to the vicious abstraction of 'feeling' from its proper context. They have accepted the terms in which both Kant and Hume saw the dispute—pitting Reason against Feeling and never asking, what sense could either make alone? What kind of motive, in particular, would 'Reason' be alone?

Kant said that reason could itself produce action; that it could be practical, and indeed that 'the will is nothing but practical Reason' (p. 75). This surprises people. How can reason have that force? Kant did not crudely overlook this question. Nor did he, as Mill thought,[9] just take it for granted that people's desire for happiness would supply the motive. He argued that a rational being could not (as a matter of *logic*) be indifferent to the fate of other rational beings. A creature which did not think of itself as one among many, a creature which did not act as such, had no respect for its fellows, attached no importance to their interests, would just not be a rational being.

The price of egoism is not just emotional solitude like Richard III's:

> I shall despair. There is no creature loves me.
> And when I die, no soul will pity me.

It is *conceptual* solitude, the collapse of thought. There is no one to talk to, no one worth arguing with, no one to agree or disagree. Not only is this very boring (after all, dislike of such solitude is supposed to be part of God's reason for creating the world) but, worse than that, Kant thought it destroyed reasoning itself—since a valid reason is one which anybody would think so, not what seems so from a single standpoint, and the notion of *anybody* requires a range of possible positions. So—no community, no reasoning. We can put this in more modern terms by saying—no language, no reasoning. And only a social being could have a language. Or again we could say—man needs fellows to find his own identity. 'Through the *Thou* a man becomes *I*.'[10] So a rational being has, by definition, to be a social being, to respect other rational beings, take them seriously, think them and their purposes important, regard them as ends and not just as means. Solipsism is not just a view that happens to be mistaken. It is mad, and so, Kant thought, we do have a *reason* to respect other people—a reason which does not depend on feeling.

He did not class as feeling the strong motives which move us to reason at all.

He did not do so, partly because he naturally thought of 'feeling' as a term for the kind of thing which the German Romantics were praising as feeling in his day and which still often monopolizes the name—floods of tears, storms of passion, love at first sight, scene and embraces, spasms of self-pity, and finally if possible, shooting oneself in despair. ('*Then* they'll be sorry. . . .')

The prime example of all these things is Goethe's novel *The Sorrows of Young Werther*, which came out in 1774, eleven years before the *Groundwork*. This book became at once the bible of the religion of feeling. Moreover, it produced a wave of suicides by shooting among young men who saw that there was at least one way in which they could imitate its hero. Kant's repeated discussion of the objections to suicide, and his choice of it as his first instance of an indulgence which mere feeling cannot justify, make sense in this context (*Groundwork* pp. 85 and 91). But apart from this question of particular applications, there is the more general and deeper one of passivity. In a sudden spasm of pity, Kant said, we are passive. It *happens* to us. In deciding to help someone on principle, we are active. And there is a quite special kind of value in the active component (pp. 88–99).

He was surely right to value it. But he over-simplified in supposing that it could conceivably occur on its own.

Every thought about values has to have its passive, contemplative element. We cannot really think injustice is bad if it does not at some point sicken us—although, as Kant rightly said, we have to go on resisting it even when that feeling intermits. (His example (p. 64) of the man who still does right even when for the time his whole capacity for feeling is absorbed by misfortunes of his own is excellent.) But, there has to be a readiness, in normal circumstances, to lay oneself open to the feelings involved; to respond emotionally in the appropriate way. The Greek (particularly Stoic) insistence on Dignity is a bad guide here. The Stoic Apathês, the man without feeling, too dignified to be moved at all by the death of his own children, is not really a specially rational being.[11] Indifference is not a conceptually proper response to this situation in such a creature as man. And mere constitutional coldness has no sort of merit at all.

Aeschylus, much less on his dignity than some Greeks, said that we learn *through suffering*.[12] He was quite right. And this is not just contingent; it is not like, say, the stimulating effect of a tonic. What we learn depends (conceptually) on the form that this particular suffering took. And it has formal connections with other states of feeling. We learn both to feel and to act differently in quite specific ways.

There is no room in Kant for the possibility that feeling may educate thought. This, of course, is what is wrong with his treatment of affection. Schiller pointed this out at once in a sharp little verse:

'Gladly I serve my friends—But I do it, alas, from affection. Hence I am plagued with doubts that I am not a virtuous person?' 'Surely the answer is clear. First you must learn to detest them. Then you can do with disgust that which the law ordains.'

Had Kant actually been the kind of foolish pedant who could possibly mean this, we could forget about him. His writing constantly shows that he was not.[13] How are we to state the truths he saw while clearly excluding this absurd corollary?

Kant does not deny that affection has value. He gives it conditional value. This groups it with such things as intelligence, resolution and ambition, things which can have great value in the right context (pp. 59 and 63–5). Their value depends on the presence of a good will. (Good will acts as a plus sign, bad will as a minus.) Now with intelligence and the rest, this seems right. As Kant says, they will not make a man good, and they can make a bad man, not only more dangerous, but actually worse, because he understands more fully just what he is doing. But will *affection* do this? (Nero loves Poppaea; both of them are unmitigated crooks; is the situation worse than it would be if neither of them cared for anybody?)[14] And what sort of a good will would that be which existed quite independent of affection for anyone? If a rational creature has to be a social creature, it has also to be a creature with affections. To suppose otherwise is an illicit abstraction.

In a human being, pure will—pure activity without any receptive, contemplative element—is arrogance, pig-headedness, blind push, deliberate arbitrariness. Calling it good will means already that it has acknowledged a value—has bowed to it, respected it, 'looked towards' it, recognized it as not to be moved away; seen, as Kant says, as 'a worth which stands in the way of Self-Love'.[15] The model of God as pure activity, as a being that need not compromise his dignity by this acceptance of values, has made it hard to see this. But people who think of God in this way do not in fact hold him out as a model for human imitation—and clearly they had better not; the point of such conceptions is to stress God's otherness, indeed his unintelligibility. Those who want to see him as more intelligible would do better, I think, to think of him neither as active nor passive, but as somehow both, transcending that contrast. The Christian tradition does in fact break with the notion of pure activity in supposing him capable of love. As Thomas Traherne put it:

It is very strange; want itself is a treasure in Heaven; and so great a one that without it there could be no treasure. God did infinitely for us, when he made us want like Gods, that like Gods we might be satisfied. The heathen deities wanted nothing, and were therefore unhappy, for they had no being. But the Lord God of Israel, the Living and True God, was from all eternity, and from all eternity wanted like a God. He wanted the communication of his divine essence, and persons to enjoy it. He wanted Worlds, He wanted Spectators, He wanted Joys, He wanted Treasures. He wanted, yet He wanted not, for He had them.

(*Centuries of Meditation*, I. 41)

In any case, Kant for one knew very well that God's position must be *formally* different from man's, and that it is utter nonsense to suppose us called upon to imitate his meta-physical status (pp. 77–8 and 95–6).

Thus to praise will without feeling makes little sense. But equally, however highly we may value feeling, we do not actually praise feeling which is divorced from will. Real affection or love, has to include steady, rational good will. That is what distinguishes it from sentimentality. It is not just a flow of emotion to which the owner is passive, like a rainstorm or the flow of bile. It has its active side. It is an *attitude*, positively endorsed by at least part of the personality. If we love in spite of ourselves, the split is *within* the personality; it is formally quite unlike having-flu-in-spite-of-ourselves. (That is why Catullus found it so agonizing.) And if someone claims to love, but shows no good will towards the person loved—entirely refuses to recognize their rights and interests—a central element in the concept of love is missing. And it is perfectly sensible to say that this 'is not love', but, for example, pride, greed, passion, vicarious ambition or senti-mentality. Examples might be the blindly possessive parent, or Herod giving orders that his wife Mariamne should be killed after his death.

And:

> love is not love
> That alters where it alteration finds
> Or bends with the remover to remove.
> (Shakespeare, Sonnet 116)

Or, of course, we can say that it *is* love, but object to that kind of love:

Why, with so evident an intention of offending and insulting me, did you choose to tell me that you liked me against your will, against your reason, even against your character?

as Elizabeth Bennett put it (*Pride and Prejudice*, Book II, chapter XI).

In short, *respect is the backbone of love*, and Kant was

absolutely right to say so. But if a vertebrate is no good without its backbone, the backbone is also little good without the rest of the creature.

Respect, for Kant, is a feeling, but a feeling distinguished by its function; by its formal properties. It is *that* feeling (whatever its actual emotional tone) by which we recognize a worth which we did not make and cannot alter; by which we concede the otherness of others. ('Respect is consciousness of a worth which thwarts my self-love.')[15] This is its mark, and so, Kant says, its importance lies in that formal characteristic and not in its appeal as a feeling. It has the same sort of importance in the practical sphere which feelings of discomfort at a confused thought and relief at a clearer one have in the theoretical sphere. It matters because of what it shows, not because of what it feels like.[16]

But the two things cannot be separated. Certainly the emotional tone of respect can vary immensely—it can be more or less reluctant, exasperated, awe-struck, astonished, puzzled or radiant—but there are limits. What sort of respect would that be whose tone was entirely that of contempt, amusement or despair? When we feel an unwilling respect, it is usually the feeling which arrives first and forces the thought. Yet to Kant *all* feelings are a contingent matter.

It is of the utmost importance . . . that we should not dream for a moment of trying to derive the reality of this principle (of duty) from the *special characteristics of human nature*. . . . Whatever . . . is derived from the special predisposition of humanity, from certain feelings and propensities . . . can give us a subjective principle—one on which we have a propensity and inclination to act—but not an objective one.

(*Groundwork* p. 88)

V   The Application of Kant's Views

So, to return to our original question—Did he really mean that it did not matter at all morally whether we hate our friends, provided that we act properly and conceal the fact sufficiently?

Taking up the pen of a frustrated novelist, Kant answers the question:

If nature had implanted little sympathy in this or that man's heart; if (being in other respects an honest fellow) he were cold in temperament and indifferent to the sufferings of others—perhaps because, being endowed with the special gift of patience and robust endurance in his own sufferings, he assumed the like in others or even demanded it; if such a man (who would in truth not be the worst product of nature) were not exactly fashioned by her to be a philanthropist, would he not still find in himself a source from which he might draw a worth far higher than any that a good-natured temperament might have?

(p. 64)

And he might—on three conditions:

1. That there is *little* sympathy in his heart, meaning rather less than others, not actually none;

2. That on *some* other important matters he does show feeling —e.g. a burning passion for justice; and

3. rather harder—that we are sure that it is only Nature (and Fate) which did the inadequate implanting; that he has not been active with the weed-killer himself.

Take 1. and 2. If he seems literally to have *no* feeling on any subject, I think we shall find him so mysterious that we shall not know how to judge him at all—we may just give up and consider him a freak. We shall hardly anyway say 'There is an exceptionally good man'. This just shows how important right and appropriate feeling is in our moral assessment of people. Kant did not make this extreme suggestion.

Again, if he feels very strongly about, e.g. justice, but never about any individual, we shall worry, because normal human feeling moves outward from the particular to the general. We have good reason to suspect Pride, Wrath, Envy or the like. For, 3., much more than in Kant's day, we shall now ask about such a man. 'How did he get like that? Is he deliberately suppressing feeling out of a fear of it?' Chronic states of feeling are not just things that happen to us, 'occur', as Moore puts it (p. 321). They express our choice. Feeling has its active, deliberate side.

Certainly indifference to other people can *come over us*. Any depression will produce it. But we can fight it. It is often perfectly possible, given time, to rouse oneself to genuinely like and mind about people. This possibility, so prominent in Kant's mind, is often dismissed as a piece of humbug on his part. But in fact it is the only defence against humbug. (Iris Murdoch gives an excellent example of this on p. 17 of *The Sovereignty of Good*). Deliberate rethinking of this kind plays a very great part in the normal development of our relations with other people. We very often have a prejudice against strangers, a prejudice which does not melt quite on its own, but which we must break down by a conscious effort at fairness.

Once our attitudes to people settle, we often forget that we ever had to make these efforts. It occurs constantly, as a completely ordinary element in our personal relations, that we reason ourselves deliberately out of a bad state of feeling.[17]

But the empiricist tradition, much more than Kant, has ignored this simple truth. Thus Moore explains that the commandment 'Thou shalt not covet' could not possibly be meant or followed literally, since people could control their stealing, but not their covetous desires. It is therefore an 'ideal rule'. I don't think that he really thought of this just as a hypothetical command, but as a sort of pious hope which might influence us indirectly—perhaps by causing different feelings to arise in us on their own. . . .?

But if we really could not control our feelings, how could we control our acts? Of course it is true that, if I must act instantly, I must act on the motives which I have now. But if I have even five minutes, I can do something about the motives too. I can see to it, for instance, that I do not shake hands with murder in my heart, but with some sort of serious attempt at good feeling. And if I fail, I have *not* succeeded in controlling my act—since the act of shaking-hands-with-murder-in-one's-heart is a different one from the alternative: doing it without. This is not just cheese-paring. Common moral consciousness will at once recognize the difference. And any more serious kind of act, such as 'advising someone' or 'looking after him when he is lonely' or indeed 'being reconciled' cannot be done at all, even in its outward manifestations, without the proper motives. (This is not just a contingent remark about the limits of human guile. The deceiver simply *will not know what to do*.) Actually, as I have suggested, only a limited range of more or less economic acts can be separated from their motives at all—and even they often only by a good deal of duplicity. (The unpleasant taste of bread-given-with-contempt has often been remarked on: it can persist even when the givers are absent.) We can only keep up this separation by carefully choosing acts cited under limited descriptions which keep them external. This means taking small examples—therefore either trivial or incomplete ones; turning away constantly from my duty to my parents or the Whole Duty of Man or the duty of procuring perpetual peace to the duty of not smoking in non-smoking carriages.[18] Such microslices of the moral life are unmanageable.

VI   Confusions About The Will

Why did Moore take this strange line? I am pretty sure that he was operating with an unrealistic notion of the will, not as practical reason, but as sorcery or blind push; one that may be described as the public school notion. (I speak as one who has suffered from being brought up on it—'You seem to have no will-power'.) He writes:

> I cannot . . . by any single act of will directly prevent from arising in my mind a desire for something that belongs to someone else, even if, when once the desire has arrived, I can by my will prevent its continuance; and even this last I can hardly do *directly* but only by forcing myself to attend to other considerations which may extinguish the desire. . . . (By contrast) the action (of stealing) is *directly* within the control of my will.
>
> (p. 316)

But attending to other things is the natural and proper way of changing one's thoughts and feelings; it is not a second-best; there is no quicker and more direct alternative. That is how 'the will' works. The 'other things' need not of course be irrelevant. When tempted to take my neighbour's bicycle, I can hold off by reminding myself how much he needs it or the like (practical reasoning). Moore's assumption that he can control the *act* directly—without any movement of the attention—depends, I think, on picking the example of theft, something he has no temptation to commit in any case. Someone who from time to time *does* steal will tell a very different story. And a better example for coveting might be *Envy* of a friend's fame and success. This coveting does not consist simply in having a sudden isolated thought, 'How I would like his position'. Moore is quite right to say that we cannot help this. It consists in welcoming, encouraging and developing that thought—instead of deliberately attending to other things, and, if that fails, tackling our meanness, and reasoning ourselves out of envy into a better state of feeling. Unless we can do that, we shall *not* in fact be able to resist saying and doing mean and spiteful things to him if we get the chance; we are on a road at whose end stands Iago. Our only other way of controlling our acts is duplicity; concealed malice. And the suggestion that there is nothing wrong about that unless it explodes into action really does stink. 'Good will' is not the power to do the right thing suddenly while still wallowing in habitual malice, envy, self-pity or the fear of life. It is the power to change such emotional habits, over time, through vigorous attending and imagining, into better ones, which will incidentally be ones from which doing the right thing becomes natural. Certainly occasional actions ahead of and contrary to one's current state of feeling are possible and necessary. As Aristotle says, someone who is trying to become just must start by doing just acts, without enjoying them. Only after practising in this way for some time will he begin to enjoy them as the just man does.[19] But this kind of thing cannot be the norm, and if constantly done, it carries the strong danger of self-deception endemic to all high spiritual pretensions. Normally, good will is utterly dependent on self-knowledge, on studying and understanding our disastrous habits of feeling. By attending to such habits *and* attending to considerations which show that they stink, we can in fact gradually control them, replacing them by better ones and feeling differently. There is nothing artificial, inhuman or bogus about this. The artificiality belongs to the other enterprise—that of trying to act correctly without attention to one's feelings. Nowell Smith gives a dreadful, though tiny, example of this; that of an 'Oxford don who disliked common-room life and whose presence caused himself and others acute distress. Yet he attended Common-Room assiduously because he thought it his duty to do so. He would have done better to stay at home.' (*Ethics*, p. 247.) Certainly. But I do not know why Nowell Smith supposes this man to be acting according to Kant. Kant's good will is the rational will; it involves a great deal of hard thinking, and this man has not thought at all; he is behaving like a fool. If he thought, he would either see that it was better to stay at home, or set about learning how to meet his colleagues and enjoy it.

We all know that it is this kind of revolution in feeling that is often required of us. Did Kant not know this? I am sure that he did, and that he took it for granted—as he safely could, since it is a common-sense point and one prominent in Christian teaching. He did not remark on it, because his whole controversial weight was thrown against sentimentalism. But I cannot find any passage where he denies it. And a famous one which has been taken as adverse really assumes this point:

It is doubtless in this sense (as a practical command) that we should understand too the passages from Scripture in which we are commanded to love our neighbour and even our enemy. For love out of inclination cannot be commanded; but kindness done from duty—although no inclination impels us, and even though natural and unconquerable disinclination stands in our way—is *practical*, not *pathological* love, residing in the will and not in the propensions of feeling, in principles of action and not of melting compassion. . . .

(p. 65)

In the first place, Kant is here talking about *enemies* and neighbours who are not friends—he is not recommending us to take this same attitude to everybody. And *some* disinclinations may be unconquerable without its following that we can never learn, by an effort, to love somebody better. In the second, 'kindness done from duty' cannot mean 'the proper actions according to the rule-book, and to hell with the state of mind'. Kindness is kindness; it has an internal component as well as an outer one. It tries to reach both outward, and inward, to grow into a mutual feeling; often it succeeds. Kant puts the point more plainly in the fuller passage in the Preface to the *Metaphysical Elements of Ethics*:

Beneficence is a duty. He who often practices this, and sees his beneficent purposes succeed, comes at last really to love him whom he has benefited.

When, therefore, it is said; Thou shalt love thy neighbour as thyself, this
does not mean, Thou shalt first of all love, and by means of that love (in the
next place) do him good; but; *Do good* to thy neighbour, and this beneficence
will produce in thee the love of men (as a settled habit of inclination to
beneficence).[20]

Actual love is required in the end. But almsgiving with hatred
or indifference in the heart is not *any* sort of love; it is not
practical love any more than pathological. Kant remarks a
little later that hatred is not just a spasm of feeling; it is a set
attitude, and therefore deliberately vicious (p. 319). And the
same would, I think, be true of contempt, dislike or even
chilly indifference—if they occurred as set attitudes to those
towards whom we recognize a duty. This becomes clearer still
in a remark made on p. 312:

Hatred of men, however, is always hateful, even though without any active
hostility it consists only in complete aversion from mankind (solitary
misanthropy). For benevolence still remains a duty even towards the
manhater, whom one cannot love, but to whom we can show kindness.

This makes it clear that in ordinary cases benevolence *ought* to
lead to actual love. That this progression should meet its
Waterloo in the occasional manhater is not surprising; Kant,
here as elsewhere, has a realistic view of the actual possibilities. But we still have a duty of kindness and benevolence
towards him and no stretching of language will reduce that to
mere outside actions.

Thought, feeling and action are conceptually, not con-
tingently, connected. They are aspects of the one thing;
conduct.

It is no use trying to unscrew the outside from the inside of
the teapot.

7 IS 'MORAL' A DIRTY WORD?

The word *moral* and its derivatives are showing signs of strain.
Like a small carpet, designed to fit a room which has been
enlarged, they are wrenched this way and that to cover the
bare spaces. Perhaps in the end we shall be forced to abandon
them altogether, as Nietzsche suggested. But this would be
wasteful, and it seems a good idea to examine first the various
spaces they can cover, and try to fix them to the one where
they are needed most. I shall approach this problem by
making very full quotations. It is not an isolated verbal puzzle
which can be settled by showing that a particular usage
exists; we need to know as well just what it is doing. There are
real muddles here, within common sense, about the relation
of thought to life. There is no simple plain-man's usage
prepared for us to follow. Anyone who uses *moral* in anything
beyond the *Daily Mirror* sense is no longer a quite plain man
anyway, and we had better follow careful writers than casual
ones, real one than imaginary ones. (Philosophers, unlike the
Erewhonians, do not have to study a hypothetical language.)
I am sure both that quotations are necessary and that mine
are inadequate; I hope other people will supplement them. As
for my choice, I can only say that I have tried very hard not to
be tendentious. Certainly I have quoted authors who are
capable of being silly and perverse, but as far as I can see the
remarks I have taken from them are sober and normal.
Anyone may disagree with them, but not, I hope, think them
idiotic or oddly worded. My point affects all the derivatives of
moral and to some extent those of ethical too, so I have drawn
my illustrations from all of them.

I shall begin with a dispute between Geoffrey Warnock and
R. M. Hare about the characteristic mark of a *moral principle*.
Hare put forward the view that a man's moral principles
simply *are* those universal principles he acts on. In reply,

Philippa Foot pointed out that not-treading-on-the-lines-of-the-paving-stones would not be a moral principle even if someone always did it and expected other people to do it.[1] She suggested that the distinguishing marks of the moral were: (1) a particular content, namely human good and harm, and (2) seriousness.[2] Suggestion (2) is the starting point of this paper. Suggestion (1), which overlaps it, was vigorously taken up by Warnock in his admirable little book *Contemporary Moral Philosophy*. Warnock went overboard for content. He said:

There are four possible 'marks' of a moral view; its psychological penumbra, its actual importance in the individual's conduct of his life; its 'universalizability'; and its general topic—human happiness or interests, needs, wants or desires . . . some form or other of the fourth is likely to turn out to be the most centrally important.

(pp. 55–7)

Warnock suggests that the three other marks are really consequences of the fourth. Our belief that a principle has a deep effect on human happiness is, he thinks, the *ground* of our thinking a special awe and respect appropriate to it, of our taking it to direct our lives, and also of our demanding it in others. These marks, if found on their own without such a belief, might be signs of obsessions, compulsion or taboo; they need not mark a moral principle. For Warnock, overriding authority is *not* a necessary mark of a moral principle:

A man might regard considerations of some kind as more important than considerations of morality, and hence might take himself, on occasion, to be *fully justified in not doing what he sincerely recognises to be right from the moral point of view* . . . [so that it is not] . . . a necessary truth that moral considerations are weightier, more important, than considerations of any other kind. (My italics.)

(p. 52)

Hare, reviewing the book [*Mind*, July 1968], took a high line. To tie morality to a content, must, he said, be arbitrary and conventional.

[In this way] . . . we might, in the end, have 'morality' neatly displayed for us in a show-case, with labels saying 'If you disagree with this you can't be making a moral judgement' . . . and yet the passers-by, though still deeply concerned about Plato's question ['how we ought to live'] might say, as many of them already do, *We don't believe in making moral judgements.'* This is the danger to which anybody is exposed who, as Warnock would like to do, founds a moral system upon a definition of morality in terms of its content. (My italics.)

(*Mind* p. 437)

(I cannot help remarking straight away that these are rather odd passers-by if they really mean, 'we don't believe in making judgements about the effect on human happiness'. They sound to me much more like people who object to making conventional judgements, or even universal judgements. However, Hare has not said what they prefer, and I shall be dealing with their predicament later.)

I think it should be plain at this point that something has gone wrong with the argument. Both parties are oversimplifying a term whose use is really quite complex. Look at the problem in a mirror:

On the planet Arret, philosophers are discussing what distinguishes the Critical Point of View. Erah, who seems behaviouristically inclined, says that to criticize *is* just constantly to flee and avoid. Toof and Kconraw say this is crude; people can avoid electric shocks and rotten cabbage, but can hardly criticize them, and can criticize plays without avoiding them. Kcronraw then suggests defining criticism not by its form but its content; perhaps artistic failure. Erah retorts that there may be deserving citizens who *do* want to criticize electric shocks; if you say 'this is simply not criticism' they will answer, 'then we are not interested in making critical judgements', and dismiss you as ossified. What I want to suggest is that Erah was right in the first place to concentrate on what criticizing *is*—the question *was* so far a formal one—but clearly wrong to think it was anything as simple as avoidance, even constant avoidance. Criticism is something both subtler and wider, involving the working out and defending of the principles on which one should choose or avoid things. We can, however, *use* what we know about content to guide us in this investigation of form. Bad art *is* a suitable thing to criticize and that fact *does* tell us something about criticism. Then we ought to be able to do as Kconraw wants and decide what is and what is not a possible object for the critical attitude, at any rate for such a creature as man (or nam). We might then show *why* it is not sense to talk about criticizing electric shocks, any more than about justifying mud or warning people against breathing, and might then approach such interesting questions as how far Job (or Boj) was in order in criticizing the Deity.

When then (to return) is the work done by calling a point of view *moral*?

I want to try the hypothesis that the *central* job the word does, the one for which it is worth preserving, is to mark, as Philippa Foot suggested, a certain sort of seriousness and importance (as in the remark, 'we can't just do what we fancy here; there is a moral question involved') and that its other implications, whether of form or content, flow from this. I therefore differ from Warnock on the point of overridingness; to my mind, if morality has a link with human happiness, it is because human happiness is an overwhelmingly important or serious matter. But I am sure he is right to look for some limit on content. I shall have to discuss more fully what 'seriousness' means here. But I must first deal with the obvious objection that 'moral', far from meaning anything like 'serious', may be taken simply as a dismissive word, or at best as a classifier restricting attention to one kind of serious consideration among many.

1 Dismissive

Macaulay said, 'We know of no spectacle so ridiculous as the British people in one of its periodical fits of morality'. Compare Mr Doolittle: 'Morals? Can't afford them governor', and Dubedat: 'Morality consists in suspecting other people of not being legally married'. The sense is strong enough to get a mention in the O.E.D. ('Moral discourse or instruction, a moral lesson or exhortation. Now chiefly in disparaging sense') and is quite old. It is the sense suggested by Hare's passers-by who don't believe in making moral judgements.

This sense is produced by humbug, a factor of enormous linguistic power. Any word much used for insincere praise ends up by being used for sincere abuse. In England *moral* etc. have had a depressing history of surfeit in the late eighteenth century, followed by nausea and nemesis in the nineteenth. But so far there is nothing peculiar in the fate of *moral*. We can speak in the same dismissive way of values we entirely accept, when they have been overpraised. ('Don't be so revoltingly fair'; 'she's so kind it make you sick'.) This is partly just reported speech; we mean that this is not proper fairness or morality; it is what passes for it with our benighted opponents. But we certainly may also be marking out the claims of competitors, noting that there are other virtues as well as fairness, *other points of view as well as the moral*. Here the disparaging use melts into:

2 Classifier

The much more general *classifying use*, which treats the moral aspect as one among many. I want to deny that this is the central use: I think it will never bear the weight of much argument, but it is common today and needs careful discussion. It is the sense suggested by my Warnock quotation. Here it is in a review by Angus Wilson:

When a young student of the novel has been so deeply steeped in the English tradition that he seems wholly given over to the social, the moral, the domestic and the humorous view of life, there are two novels, I think, that may effect a cure.

(*Observer*, July 1970)

Here the moral shrinks to a very small province indeed. In the same way, it often finds itself opposed to some form of the expedient. Thus a typical example from any paper might read:
(Sentence X) 'Morally, the case for helping these people is unanswerable; the sad thing is that politically/economically/in practice nothing can be done.'

I ignore the dull case where nothing *can* be done; if so, the whole thing is just an expression of regret. Barring this, *what sort of a distinction is it that is being made between the provinces?* Is it a true classification, a final, complete division between co-ordinate realms? ('He is not Dutch but Austrian.' 'This is not red but green.') Does it allow of no further arbitration procedure? Must we choose our standpoint by an inexpressible leap in the dark, as Sartre or even Hare might suggest? If it turns out to be so, we shall be at a great disadvantage, since thought and discussion will no longer help us. It seems sensible to go on trying arbitration until it is proved not to work (which has certainly not been done yet) rather than insist on waiting till it is proved that it will. The burden of proof is on the divider.[3]

Suppose, then, that there *is* some proper arbitration procedure between viewpoints. If so, Sentence X is not meant to be a final, satisfactory classification, but to mark a dilemma. ('Toads have lungs, and these things seem to be toads, but dammit, where are their lungs?') Warnock, unlike Hare, thinks there *is* a procedure, since he says that the agent, '*thinks it best* not to act as his moral principle requires' and, 'might take himself to be *fully justified* in not doing what he sincerely recognises to be right from the moral point of view'.

What kind of reasoning does he use to do this? We can't call it *moral* reasoning; we must find or invent some other name. We might call it 'intersectional reasoning' morality being one of the sections. Or we might say 'judicial reasoning', morality being one of the litigants. These terms suggest a neutral standpoint, a supreme position with no bias towards any of the claimants. Is any such standpoint conceivable? Federal superpowers are awkward enough in politics; their status is puzzling both theoretically and practically; does anyone think it would be easier in psychology?

I may seem to press the spatial or political metaphor of *provinces* and *points of view* too crudely, but my whole project is to investigate these metaphors. They are seldom unpacked. It is ludicrous to assume a final separation between 'points of view' when, as we know, dispute between them goes on perpetually both inside us and without, and is quite often fruitful. What actually happens in such cases does not seem to be either external arbitration or (except when we are lazy or time presses) an unspeakable leap in the dark. Instead, we develop the two contending forms of reasoning until they turn out to have terms in common. After that, both forms will be altered, and a system formed which to some extent accommodates both. Without this, we cannot choose. With it, we have a further system, and we want to know what to call it. Is there, as things stand, a better name than 'a morality'? I only ask for information.

The trouble is that, alongside the sectional classifying use of *moral* there already is an inclusive one, for which Morality is either the central province of the inner life or the federation, the total system of values inside which the provinces fit. This use may sound less English than the other; here are two striking instances from extraneous sources, both given by the O.E.D.

1 A bill of indemnity . . . for raid by Dr. Jameson and the British South African Company's troops, the account falls under two headings:

> First: Material damage, Total claim   £577,938. 3. 3.
> Second: Moral or intellectual damage,   Total claim of £1,000,000.
> (Paul Kruger, as reported to the House of Commons by J. Chamberlain.)

2 In war, moral considerations make up three quarters of the game; the relative balance of man-power accounts for the remaining quarter. (Napoleon's correspondence.)

But in fact this usage is as English as any other; it is only that in English other uses have lately had more of the philosophical limelight. English writers used it in just this way, without a hint of embarrassment, up to the mid-eighteenth century. Even Hume, with his powerful nose for humbug, never hesitated to speak of moral essays, moral sentiments, moral faculties, moral good and evil. It seems to have been the sentimental piety of the late eighteenth century that brought forward the debased complimentary use (*'truly* moral sentiments'), and put off the sensitive. Doctor Johnson had much to do with this sad development, catching the word at its forking point and pinning it firmly to outward observance of simple conventional rules (as in the phrase 'his morals') and to retributive justice (as in 'the moral of the tale'). It is worth looking closely into Johnson's treatment of the words to see the climate in which this external, practical, behaviouristic sense, now so popular with philosophers, took shape, and I propose to do so. Those who consider that history is bunk may skip to p. 114.

Johnson in his *Dictionary* gave as the first sense of *moral*, 'Relating to the Practice of men towards each other, as it may be virtuous or criminal, good or bad'. His examples do not really support this sense at all, but it is still his first choice. And what he takes it to say about the practice of men towards each other is that it is ruled by retributive justice. That is clear from a hundred passages, notably this from the Preface to his Shakespeare;

[Shakespeare's] first defect is that to which may be imputed most of the evil in books or men. He sacrifices virtue to convenience, *he seems to write without any moral purpose.* . . . . *He makes no just distribution of good and evil*, nor is careful to show in the virtuous a disapprobation of the wicked. . . . This fault the barbarity of his age cannot extenuate for *it is always a writer's duty to make the world better*, and justice is a virtue independent on time and place.

Nor was this his last word on the subject. Ten years later, Boswell raised the matter again:

I objected the great defect of the tragedy of Othello was, that it had not a moral, . . . for that no man could resist the circumstances of suspicion which were artfully suggested to Othello's mind.

Johnson: In the first place, Sir, we learn from Othello this very useful moral, not to make an unequal match, in the second, we learn not to yield too readily to suspicion. . . . No Sir, I think Othello has more moral than almost any play.[4]

Taking one thing with another, this seems to be one of the worst missed opportunities in the history of criticism. Johnson

drove a quite unnecessary wedge between the moral and the
aesthetic standpoint, and did all he could to make it seem
impenetrable. He thought very highly of Shakespeare; he
praised him soundly for his truth to nature, yet he could not
see that a moral defence too was available.[5] For instance: that
a dramatist's moral stature or purpose does not depend on
enforcing a prefabricated rule, much less on enforcing it by
telling lies about retributive justice. The dramatist's business
is to use moral insight, to see, not only how people think and
act, but how good and bad such thoughts and actions can be.
He points out to us certain splendours and miseries; in
general it is for us to make any practical applications that
may follow. Sometimes, if we believe him, certain practical
applications plainly *will* follow; then we call him a moralist as
well as a dramatist or novelist. But there is no guarantee that
the moral drawn will agree with existing moral views; it may
or it may not. He may turn out (tiresome fellow) to be an
unacknowledged legislator of mankind, in which case it is no
use asking him to police the laws he is replacing. And even
where the practical application is plain, the core of the
moralist's business will be something beyond it. This is the
change he makes in our inner lives, in the way that we see
things. Thus: what makes Aeschylus a moralist is his attack
on the savage traditional Greek vendetta theory of justice, an
attack on its spirit as well as its practice; what makes him a
great moralist is his immense courageous insight into the
whole problem of suffering and its place in human life. You
could have learnt Aeschylus' lesson even if you never had the
least occasion to adjudicate a blood-feud, you could have
learnt it even if from some chance or other you never *did*
anything you would not in any case have done, but only
viewed everything differently. And you certainly would *not*
have learnt it if you had only imbibed (say by aversion
therapy) the practical precept—'Avoid vendettas', even
supported by the belief 'vendettas do not pay'.

Thus a writer's moral significance is quite independent of
the sort of thing Johnson pegged it to: *unless* you take moral in
the narrow sense he preferred. Why should you do so?
Johnson himself had excellent reasons. Johnson was no
hypocrite; he was a man haunted, terrified, obsessed by the

fear of Hell. Morality for him was a fixed code of practice imposed from without by God; it was our only safeguard against eternal torture, and it was made effective, not by being understood, but *only* by the threat of punishment, temporal and eternal. He did not believe any other persuasion could in the least be relied on. Again and again he insists that the character of an infidel is more detestable than that of a man guilty of an atrocious crime, 'for the infidel would be guilty of any crime if he were inclined to it'.[6] Nothing withholds us but fear, first of the jail, then of damnation. Puzzled by this, someone once asked him 'what he meant by being damned?' Johnson broke out in agony, 'Sent to Hell, Sir, and punished everlastingly.'[7] This was the fear he lived in; he was occupied with his own sin, not other people's, which is what gives such dreadful force to his insistence on the autonomy of morals as he understood it. He had no confidence in any general moral enquiry, any psychological or metaphysical quest for the roots of moral practice. There could be no such roots. This is what made it seem impossible for us to improve on existing rules by a better understanding of human nature, and determined the comment drawn from him by Boswell's piteous case-history of the ill-treated lady: 'My dear Sir, never accustom your mind to mingle virtue and vice. The woman's a whore, and there's an end on't.'[8] This is what makes it impossible to trust the most respectable agnostic (such as Hume).

I do not say that Johnson thought like this all the time. Nobody does so; you could hardly stay sane if you did. Nor do I claim to have compressed the very complex history of the word into this one example. I use Johnson, this official Johnson, as a sad example of the motives for overstressing the practical sense of the word, and of what happens when you do. His actual usage, of course, is inconsistent. He has the word in all sorts of other sense, including Kant's,[9] and he is sometimes willing to give quite subtle reasons for the practices he approves. He uses blunderbusses like 'there's an end on't' just as the rest of us do, to mean, 'I can't be bothered to argue that with *you*' or 'to argue it this evening', or, very often 'you know that as well as I do.' Nevertheless, to treat most sorts of argument as actually irrelevant is his official line, and for someone with his beliefs official lines do have a particular importance. If conformity is what we need for salvation, standing up to be counted for the right may actually be more important than living up to it. So Johnson, much though he hated humbug, could praise Savage for recommending in his writings the virtues that he never practised.[10] This is a pretty sophisticated point. Yet Johnson is always thought of as a champion of common sense against sophistication. Echoes of him are heard whenever Moore and Prichard are in their common-sense plain-man mood. ('Good is good and that is the end of the matter!')[11] And Johnson's line *is* common sense —provided you happen to believe in eternal damnation without explanation. In the context of that sort of Protestantism, all other sorts of reasons for adopting principles do pale into insignificance beside their effect on our own and other people's salvation. In that context, the ingenious speculations of the Enlightenment about the foundations of morals do become, not only irrelevant, but maddening. ('Truth, Sir, is a cow that will yield such people [Hume and Rousseau] no more milk, so they are gone to milk the bull.')[12] But, of course, explanation as such is not abandoned; it is only that one sort of explanation is preferred to all others. No one before Prichard ever suggested doing without explanation altogether. No man, however plain, who can think at all, really thinks that morality consists *only* in practice. To mention practice apart from spirit and intention is meaningless abstraction.

It was in this way that Johnson, and the men of his age, pegged the word *moral* to the narrow sense of Outside Regularity, moved by a distrust of (non-religious) thought and a powerful fear of damnation. Just at the same time, Kant pegged it to intention, and not to isolated intention either but to a man's whole framework of principles. Only when an agent's motive is the right one *'would his conduct first acquire full moral worth'*[13] for Kant. For him *'imitation has nothing to do with morality'*.[14] Yet of course imitation—the speciality of the conventional man, the wily hypocrite and the zombie—can produce faultless outside regularity. You don't find *them* smoking in the wrong railway carriage. The two usages are almost exactly opposite.

In English philosophy, the Johnsonian one prevailed. Mill, marking out the liberty of the individual conscience, did not say, as he might have done, 'Society had no right to interfere in moral affairs'. He said that morality, meaning social control, must not interfere in private affairs. It is only when there is danger of damage to others that 'the case is taken *out of the province of liberty and placed in that of morality or law*'.[15] And for Mill, too, punishment is a sure mark of the moral. 'We do not call anything wrong unless we mean that a person ought to be punished in some way for doing it. . . . This seems the real turning-point of the distinction between morality and simple expediency.'[16] This is a most confusing use. But where Mill left the term, there, as though Nietzsche had never lived, Moore picked it up. As it has turned out, this decision has surely been disastrous, because both punishment and outward regularity are ideas which have taken a terrible beating in the hundred years since Mill, and so far as moral is bound to them, it cannot help becoming a dirty word. It has, in fact, become far more discredited, far harder to use in English as a result of this debasement than it seems to have on the Continent as a result of Nietzsche's direct attacks on it.

1. To deal first briefly with punishment and its relation to morality. Here, most of us now, I take it, would agree with Wittgenstein (I quote Wittgenstein, though the point was first made by Glaucon and Adeimantus):[17]

> When an ethical law of the form of 'Thou shalt . . .' is laid down, one's first thought is, 'And what if I do not do it?' It is clear however that ethics has nothing to do with punishment or reward in the usual sense of the terms. So our question about the *consequences* of an action must be unimportant. At least those consequences should not be events. For there must be something right about the question that we posed. There must indeed be some sort of ethical reward and ethical punishment, but they must reside in the action itself.
>
> (And it is also clear that the reward must be something pleasant and the punishment something unpleasant).
>
> (*Tractatus Logico-Philosophicus* 6.422)

Wittgenstein here attempts what Johnson refused to attempt, namely to make sense of punishment by internalizing it. The punishment for doing X is, perhaps, becoming the

sort of person who does things like X—perhaps simply
becoming the person who *did* do X and has to live with the
memory. (In the same way some Christians now regard Hell
as simply the state of separation from God.) Punishment does
not lose its importance if you look at things in this way, but it
does become a secondary and dependent moral concept,
needing for its sense an independent understanding of what it
is to do wrong. It cannot possibly be used to *define* the moral
sphere, as Mill suggested.

2. As for the notion of morality as outward observance, its
current form is the view that moral principles deal with
classes of outward acts, 'One ought never to smoke in
compartments where there is a No Smoking notice' or 'never
say what is false, except in war-time to deceive the enemy'.[18]
This is the taboo sense, the sense in which Nietzsche understood and attacked the concept of morality.

It is not my business here to ask whether this behaviouristic
formula is ever a possible form for a moral principle, but
simply to point out that it is not the only possible form. Moral
principles take innumerable other forms, for instance, 'Honour
thy father and thy mother'; 'People are more important than
things', 'Charity is more important than Faith or Hope'; 'a
man's life is not his own'. Or with Langland:

> Chastity without Charity lieth chained in Hell
> It is a lamp with no light in it.

That being so, I want to ask why the word 'moral' got pegged
so easily to the external imperative formula. And the
melancholy answer lies in the tradition I have traced. Where
Mill put down the word *moral*, there, in its Johnsonian
pigeon-hole, Moore picked it up, and where Moore put it,
there, regardless of intelligent usage, it has stayed. Moore
always uses it for outward regularities of this kind, though he
dropped the interest in punishment which gave a sense to this
externality. He often uses it with a shade of impatience,
because he rightly thinks that outward regularity is not the
whole duty of man, but with a wholly unjustified air of being
the first to say so.[19]

Everybody knows that moral teachers are largely concerned in laying down moral rules, and in disputing the truth of rules which have been previously asserted. And moral rules seem to consist, to a very large extent, in assertions to the effect that it is always wrong to do certain actions, or to refrain from doing certain others.

Does everyone know that? Which moral teachers are these? Moore says explicitly that they rule on *external* actions. Is there any set of moral teachers *largely* concerned with ordering or forbidding these? Not all of the Ten Commandments do it, though Moore thought they did. Stealing and murder are not defined in at all the same external way as smoking in railway carriages; they depend on the very complicated concepts of property and intention, and they cover a vast variety of external acts.[20] In fact, pulpit moralists and popular sages alike, and certainly all moral philosophers, have been far more interested in dozens of other questions; in *why* the things already known to be wrong or right were so; in the different ways and degrees of their rightness, in questions about the nature of the world and the soul, in arguments for settling disputes about what was right, in destiny and individuality, in human motivation, in temptation, effort and choice, in ideals and purposes, in God, freedom and immortality. That is, of course, they have always been what Moore forbade them to be, psychologists and metaphysicians. They have dealt in thought as well as action. They have to. People will not obey orders without explanations. Even if a moralist himself were only interested in reform, he would have to enter into his hearers' natural curiosity about the background and reasons for it, if he wanted to be obeyed. I can only think that Moore came to the view quoted by ignoring in his predecessors' work all he thought had no business to be there. Or possibly he himself was using *moral* in a contemptuous or dismissive sense, meaning 'crudely moralistic or pulpit-bashing'. He makes another very strange remark in the same paper, saying of the 'central idea of Aristotle's Ethics'—the good at which all things aim—that it is 'not a moral idea at all' though it is still 'an idea which it is the business of moral philosophy to discuss'. (*Phil. Studies* p. 326.) Ambiguities of this sort never bothered Moore, but it is time they bothered the rest of us.

Official British philosophy, then, has stuck to the narrow external behaviouristic sense of *moral*. But alongside this narrow sense, the old, useful general one has persisted. It is very common in such quiet, unemphatic phrases as; moral courage, moral feebleness, moral commitment, moral obtuseness, moral support. It is much like *spiritual*, but without the ontology. The main antithesis—moral versus material—has been enriched by several others—moral versus legal, intellectual, supernatural, conventional—and in these cases *moral* appears on the inward, the more central and personal side of the dividing line (not on the outer, as it does when opposed to 'faith' or 'emotion'). It means more, however, than just *inner*, because it conveys that these qualities—the moral courage, obtuseness or what not—belong to the whole person; they are not just chancy, they connect with his principles and his system of values. The nearest synonyms are phrases like 'strength or weakness *of character*'. (*Moral* in this sense has in fact much closer connections with *mores* = character, than with *mos* = custom—which is the favourite sense of British academic discussions.) In this way it actually comes to mean 'comprehensive, affecting the whole man'; an emphatic sense, nearly opposite to the sectional, dismissive one. The word 'moralist' generally follows this sense, leaving 'morals' and 'immorality' as the strongholds of the other.

Examples
1. 'He wanted, he was saying, life to have a moral beginning and middle and end. He wanted to form part of a pattern.' (Rebecca West, *The Thinking Reed*, ch. XII).
2. (Girls who married one man when they loved another deceived themselves about it) 'so that they became incapable of distinguishing between truth and untruth, lost their moral weight, and flickered in life without any foothold in reality'. (Isak Dinesen, *Winter's Tales* p. 115).

The job this word does is an essential job. If one talks of provinces there must be a name for the whole country, if one talks of points of view there must be a way to walk between them. Could another word than *moral* be used? There are reasons for wishing so, particularly the association with humbug. But it is useless changing the word while the

ambivalence remains. If you call rat-catchers 'rodent officers'
to dispel prejudice, you will soon have to call rodent officers
'Pest Control Operatives' and be no further forward.

Let us try and see how it is that *Moral*, like *Art* and *America*,
is the name both of a part and of the whole.

The great reason is that *moral* when used merely to classify,
to mark off one aspect among others, sounds paradoxical and
inadequate the moment you really think about it. An isolationist morality is a bad morality. We certainly do distinguish a man's moral principles from (say) his aesthetic,
sporting or religious principles. But if that distinction is final,
if there is no relation between them, we think the worse, in a
general way, of him and them; we have a *moral* objection to
the arrangement. This is crystal clear in the case of the oldest
and commonest of these distinctions, the sense to which *moral*
would certainly be confined if we went by Common Language
and the Plain Man; namely, the distinction between sexual
and other kinds of vice and virtue. Euphemism is responsible
for this one. People would rather say *moral* than *sexual*; they
would rather say *sin* or *immorality* than mention whatever
special variety of the unmentionable is on hand at the time.
This narrow use is highly distorting, and conflicts with the
wider sense which is more useful and quite as natural. George
Eliot devoted a whole essay to shooting it down. [*Impressions of
Theophrastus Such ch. 16, Moral Swindlers*]:

Yet I find even respectable historians of our own and of foreign countries,
after showing that a king was treacherous, rapacious, and ready to sanction
gross breaches of the administration of justice, end by praising him for his
pure moral character. . . . And since we are often told of such maleficent
kings that they were also religious, *we arrive at the curious result that the most
serious, wide-reaching duties of man lie quite outside both morality and religion*—the
one of these consisting in not keeping mistresses (and perhaps in not
drinking too much) and the other in certain ritual and spiritual transactions
with God, which can be carried on equally well side by side with the basest
conduct towards men.

I have italicized the point I want to stress here; there is really
something curious, something paradoxical, about treating
morality as an isolated province. Once the point is raised, we

can hardly go on saying, 'from the moral point of view, good; from the humane point of view, abominable' and leave it at that. Partial moral systems must expand or die. There is an interesting asymmetry here among the various alleged provinces of value. If you want to say that a man is wholly given over to any one of them, you can do it by saying that:

Art,
Sport,
Finance,
Politics,
Psycho-analysis   } is his religion or morality,
Fashion
Medicine
The Stage
Research etc., etc.

but I do not think you can say that religion or morality is any of the others. You sometimes get an intelligible proposition if you try, but it is a different one. The nearest alternative might be to say that art etc. was his whole life, which is significant enough. But even this states a fact rather than a claim. Only morality and religion carry the connection with justification, suggesting 'that by which he thinks he ought to test everything else'. (I can say nothing here about the gap between morality and religion; obviously they are sometimes opposed, but used in the way I have just mentioned I think they run parallel.) The two of them differ from other partial systems in that they cannot be put into subordinate positions without degrading them entirely. (This is where I disagree with Warnock.) If X admits that smearing his opponent with a false charge is immoral, but justifies it on political grounds, you cannot, to my mind, say that he has a perfectly good morality, which isn't relevant to this purely political question. You can either say that his morality turns out to be idle taboo and convention, or that his real morality is a political one, which need not be an insult. Just so, if we take religion in the sense it now bears in Western life, it is hardly possible to say that a brutal traitor is, from the religious point of view, completely admirable. Empire-building, which is an inclination of all systems, is of the definition of these two. They cannot accept a minor position and survive. Morality has no alternative but to make Butler's terrifying claim: 'Had it strength, as it has right; had it power, as it has manifest authority, it would absolutely govern the world' (Sermon 2). It demands in all cases to govern such a creature as man. Hence the puzzle, hence the ambivalence, hence the impression of humbug. People who revolt against existing moral terms cannot, if they want to be positive, abandon moral terms entirely. Time and again they hurl the name in the mud, only to pick it up, wash it carefully, and lay claim to it, along with its peculiar tone and its apparatus of virtue, merit, sin, conscience and responsibility, as a perquisite of their own higher principles. Immoralists are after all only a species of moralists.

Examples
1.

There is no such thing as a moral or an immoral book. Books are well written or badly written. . . . The moral life of man forms part of the subject matter of the artist; but the *morality of art* consists in the perfect use of an imperfect medium.

(Oscar Wilde, Introduction to *Dorian Gray*)

The useful phrase 'the morality of x' deserves attention. It means, 'x taken as a system of value'; 'x taken as binding'. It is a perfectly sensible phrase, not like 'the red of green'. If one spoke, conversely, of 'the art of morality', one might also be intelligible, but one would not convey the binding element.

2.

Tanner: Morality can go to its father the devil. . . . [later, describing his own adolescence], No; the change that came to me was the birth of moral passion; and I declare that according to my experience moral passion is the only real passion.
Ann: All passions ought to be moral, Jack.
Tanner: Ought! Do you think that anything is strong enough to impose oughts on a passion except a stronger passion still?

Ann: Our moral sense controls passion Jack. Don't be stupid.
Tanner: Our moral sense! And is not that a passion? . . . the mightiest of
the passions. It is the birth of that passion that turns a child into a man.
. . . That passion dignified (his other passions) gave them conscience and
meaning, found them a mob of appetites and organized them into an
army of purposes and principles. My soul was born of that passion.

(Shaw, *Man and Superman*, Act 1)

3.

Don Juan The confusion of marriage with morality has done more to
destroy the conscience of the human race than any other error. . . . [To the
devil] Your friends are the dullest dogs I know. . . . They are not religious,
they are only pewrenters. They are *not moral, they are only conventional.* They
are not virtuous; they are only cowardly. . . . To be in hell is to drift; to be in
heaven is to steer.

(*ibid*: Act 3)

That whole scene is devoted to the distinction between
'True Morality' and the conventional code. There could have
been no better chance for Shaw to have discarded the *term*
morality with the rest of the lumber if he had wanted to—he
had already shied several tomatoes at it. But how was he to
get on without it? What else could he use? He still had a
system of values to defend, 'an army of purposes and
principles'. (I have actually heard an anarchist remark
indignantly 'Well it's *always* wrong to make moral judgements', but there are difficulties in following up this move.)
Even Nietzsche performed the same sort of manoeuvres,
though he was much quicker on his feet.

4.

We immoralists! . . . We are spun into a strict network and hairshirt of
duties: we cannot get out. In this we are men of duty, even we.

(*Beyond Good and Evil*, Sec. 226. Cf. Sec. 228—
'Isn't moralising . . . immoral?')

Without a comprehensive morality you are not only unable
to direct other people—one might put up with that—you are

unable to direct yourself; it is not only that others can't understand you; you can't understand yourself. And Shaw's morality is certainly meant to be a comprehensive one; what offends him about the conventional code is exactly its patchy, parochial, sectional character. *A morality that accepts a subordinate place is dead and will soon stink*; let Michael Frayn's computer-man pronounce its epitaph;

Let's accept . . . that all ethical systems are ossified, in which case all operations within an ethical system can be performed by computer. I should be designing circuits to demonstrate what happens when one ossified system, say a Christian one, comes in contact with another ossified system, say a liberal agnostic one. And what happens when two computers with incompatible systems try to program a third between them. . . . These vast, petrified forests are our rightful domain. They are waiting helplessly to be brought under the efficient, benevolent rule of the kindly computer.

(*The Tin Men*, pp. 122–3)

But the need for a live morality still remains.

So far I have shown examples where what is at first opposed to morality and later absorbed into it is a personal standard—psychological, aesthetic, spiritual; something more intimate than the conventional code. What about standards which are more public?

I return now to Sentence X ('Morally the case for helping these people is unanswerable; the sad thing is that politically/economically/in practice nothing can be done.') Will anyone at this time of day claim that the moral has no link with these branches of the expedient? Is anyone a Political or Economic Man all the time? Of course the different aspects sometimes *strike* us separately, so that we call them different points of view, but it is no harder to find one's way between them than it is between geographical viewpoints. What looks round from the north and south, but oblong from the east and west, is not some monstrous enigma, fragmenting our concepts of space; it is a cylinder, perhaps a large drain-pipe. Mill showed how to deal with Sentence X. He didn't use the word *moral*, because he had confined it to the narrow sense, but that doesn't affect his argument.[21]

The Expedient, in the sense in which it is opposed to the Right, generally means that which is expedient to the particular interest of the agent himself. . . . When it means anything better than this, it means that which is expedient for some immediate object, some temporary purpose, but which violates a rule whose observance is expedient in a much higher degree.

So when we say that political or economic considerations forbid us to help these people, though morality commands it, we may simply mean (1) that we ought to do it, but we are not going to because it would cost too much. This is intelligible and honest, but it is not a justification. Or (2) we may mean that our duty to our own citizens actually overrides our duty to help the foreign claimants. This *is* a justification (successful or not) and it is a moral one. So now the moral case is not given up as unanswerable. In the same way, if we happen here to be dealing with one of the moral ideals which cannot be stated in utilitarian terms as easily as Mill supposed, it is still a moral dispute that is going forward, because that ideal is set against the moral ideal of promoting happiness. Economic and political considerations are only partial, abstract purposes, waiting to be set against the others, they only make sense as part of a wider system, and that system only makes sense when it includes them. The right is not an isolated property, object of an unaccountable taboo, not a peculiar colour effect visible only from a peculiar viewpoint. Nor is the expedient something only visible from a peculiar viewpoint. To call something either right *or* expedient is already to say that one has visited the relevant viewpoints and made a calculation which allows for their divergence. It is not a bit like saying it glimmers or looks pink from the house; it is much more like saying it is round or square.[22] And having got that far, one can calculate some more and account for the apparent divergence. Compare this (*The Guardian*, 23 July 1970): 'Mr. Hain added, "The time for sterile, violent confrontrations—bumping policemen in Grosvenor Square—is over. They were seen to be *not only politically but morally sterile*. I have sufficient belief in non-violent militancy to believe it can be carried out in a non-violent fashion."' I take it this means, 'not only did they make us enemies; they were out of tune with what we were trying to do'. Mr. Hain's 'not only' marks his view of the hierarchy of values. He means that it is *worse* to be doing something incompatible with your main purpose than merely to find obstacles in your way. This is the sort of priority system which Mill suggested for dealing with conflicts of rights and interests, and whatever may be wrong with Mill's own list of priorities, something of the sort is indispensable. If one takes up the alternative of a meaning for right [or for moral] so autonomous as to say nothing about advantage, the term is degraded at once into mere Musical Bank currency, talked of and displayed on Sundays, but known not to be the slightest use for paying anybody [no good, as Sentence X so oddly has it, 'in practice']. No serious moral philosopher has ever proposed such a morality. Kant is sometimes accused of doing so by people who have skipped through the *Groundwork of the Metaphysics of Morals*; a glance at the *Critique of Practical Reason* would dispel the idea. If it follows from the above remarks that Prichard was not a serious moral philosopher, I have no objection.

My main suggestion should now be becoming clear. I said that the central job done by 'moral', the job for which it was worth preserving, was to mark a certain sort of seriousness and importance, as in the remark, 'we can't just do what we fancy here; there is a moral question involved'. I have now tried to show how the word becomes fitted for this job, how it can mean 'belonging to a man's character, to his central system of purposes', and I have argued that the job is an essential one. I have suggested that Johnson's alternative of pinning it to certain recognized practices is a dead end. I have said that I do not at all mind another word being substituted for moral if anyone can find a better one, but that I suspect any other word will at present run into the same sort of problems. To develop the suggested meaning further, I shall now ask, *what is this special kind of seriousness or importance?*

What is a serious matter?

A serious matter is one that affects us deeply. This is not the same as giving us a strong sensation; a sudden violent toothache which never recurs is not a serious matter, nor is the taste of pepper, whereas a persistent apathy, an absence of all strong sensations, would be very serious indeed. Not everything with lasting effects will qualify; a chronic complaint need not be serious. This is interesting; we can say, 'Yes, his rheumatism is bad, it would be serious for some people but it really isn't for him'. If his purposes in life do not involve much moving around, rheumatism is not serious; if he is a dancer, a sore toe may be. What is serious affects something central among his systems of purposes and it is that system we need to know about. Its variation, however, has limits. Any approach to total paralysis, total solitude, total destituion, total monotony, total confusion, universal hostility, is serious for anybody. You cannot claim that it is not so for a particular person simply as an odd fact, without giving an explanation, and it will have to be a good one. It is no use for instance simply saying, 'he chooses not to care about it'. Explanation will have to move by describing an exceptional history, exceptional alternatives, and thereby a readiness to use an exceptional substitute for normal needs. ('He needs no human company because he talks with God/he lives in the past/he prefers seagulls/he is off his head anyway and can only talk to himself.') All this will be met with justified scepticism at first, melting only when we have grasped the complete picture of an accepted way of life. The same thing, of course, will be true if we are told that what *is* serious for him is the behaviour of a spider. Unless we are told *how* spiders come to matter so much (he is an entomologist, he is a spider-worshipper, he is Robert the Bruce) this is simply unintelligible, because seriousness involves connections with what is *naturally important for a human being*. This point seems needlessly complicated because many people, such as sociologists and existentialists, like to claim officially that there is no such thing as human nature, so that nothing is naturally any more important than anything else. This means that [for instance] total immobility or total solitude would be as good ways of life as any other, provided you either were brought up to them or decided to choose them. Man is supposed to be infinitely plastic. I think this aspiration towards total openness is at the back of Hare's refusal to tie morality to a content.

I find this contention so obscure (even a piece of plasticine is not *infinitely* plastic; everything has *some* internal structure) that I propose simply to wait till I find someone living by it;

i.e. choosing such things, refraining from ever mentioning or appealing to human nature or instinct, not treating anything as naturally more important than anything else, avoiding Freudian argument, and (in particular) finding a way to reconcile their views with the actual behaviour of babies, before I start taking trouble about it. The fashion for infinite plasticity seems in fact to be on the way out in the social sciences. Meanwhile, I propose to take it that we *are* so constituted as to mind more about some things than about others; that these distinctions can to some extent be traced, however much they are overlaid by training; that it is only among these things that we can make an intelligible choice; that an unintelligible choice is no choice at all, and that a connection with these things is of the essence of seriousness.

Now what happens if we ask; *is it not only a serious but a moral matter?* My short and wild answer is that *moral* is simply the superlative of serious. Provided we are talking practically—talking about what people choose to do, think and be, not just about what happens to them—anything that affects their central purposes deeply is a moral matter, any choice of central purpose is a moral choice, because it involves what any one will call moral thinking. To move house need hardly affect one's central purposes at all; to move from country to town may affect them quite a lot, because it means giving priority to different friends and occupations; to pass the rest of one's life in solitude in a space-craft would certainly do so. Doing that would therefore be a moral decision. I do not think there is, outside the text books, a hard and fast line fixed round the moral. Seriousness is a matter of degree, and if a thing is certainly very serious, however little connexion it may seem to have with the conventional code, we rightly call it a moral matter. But of course this is not the end of the story, because a morality cannot be private whatever else can, and if anybody claims that some unexpected thing is either *very serious* or *a moral question* to him, he has got to explain what his system of purposes is and how this comes into it, otherwise we shall not understand him. The claims an art seems to have on an artist, or a science on a scientist have been made explicit by now—my quotations from Wilde show the early stages of the process. *Are they moral claims?* If the claimant makes good sense of the system of purposes put forward, yes. Suppose the dancer, the violinist, the astronomer or the mathematician are poor; they are faced with the choice of abandoning their art, debasing it, or asking someone else for money. Suppose the Philistine pours scorn on the idea that they could have a moral problem: his line will be that these matters fall outside morality. To reach this point I suggest that he will naturally argue that they are *unimportant, trivial, not serious.* (He may well put this in the form 'they do not affect the general happiness', but this will only work if we know first that only what affects the general happiness is important.) Can he be answered? He *must* be; he is inside us as well as outside. Various answers are possible, and they too all take the route through the concept of seriousness to show a moral claim. We may say for instance: *this matters because what matters most for everybody is the exercise of his faculties.* We can argue, with Aristotle[23] and Mill,[24] that this exercise is at the root of the concept of happiness itself, and therefore of the general happiness. A man who betrays his central talent loses his soul.

> to thine own self be true,
> And it shall follow, as the night the day,
> Thou canst not then be false to any man.
> (*Hamlet*, Act I, sc. iii)

This point is often put in terms of integrity, and integrity is clearly a traditional moral virtue. (See nearly all of Angus Wilson's novels, and particularly *Anglo-Saxon Attitudes*, where everything revolves round the integrity of the scholar.) Again, we can point out that *the arts and sciences have a public*, so that watching or learning dancing etc. might really form part of the general happiness. But we shall then have to show that they form an important, a serious part, and are not just replaceable candy floss. This again we may do by Aristotelian arguments about the importance of developing people's latent sensibilities. (We shall need a psychological theory to back this.) We can speak in religious terms of the Parable of the Talents, of Mary and Martha and of Our Lady's Juggler, etc.—but that will only work if we can make plausible on its own the view which we are attributing to God—namely that

the use of people's central talents is an important matter. And
so on. I do not at all want to suggest that these arguments
about integrity must always be successful. I think in fact that
they have been over-inflated by fashion and need to be
brought back into relation with plenty of others. Integrity is
certainly not the whole of virtue. What I do say is that they
call on a perfectly workable set of concepts, *which have become
continuous with the concepts of traditional morality, by making out their
claim to be serious. After that, morality excludes them at its peril.* In
the same way, a choice between Homeric and modern ideals
would be a moral choice; and Nietzsche when he recom-
mended the Homeric set was forced in spite of himself to
present it as such.[25] He could not simply impose Bronze Age
standards on his contemporaries; he had to justify and defend
them in modern terms, and to use one modern ideal to upset
another, all of which is moral argument. But for the Homeric
Greeks themselves no problem arose. They pursued the only
things they thought could possibly be important. I think it is
this, not, as Warnock suggests (p. 54) the content of their
ideals, which makes us hesitate to call them moral, but the
fact that they conceive of no alternative. (Hector, if he is taken
to *argue* with Andromache, might possibly be an exception. . . .?)[26] Any modern writer recommending a return to
the primitive runs into Nietzsche's problem—the deliberately
revived ideal differs *formally* from its model just because it is
consciously chosen and defended, however closely it may
imitate the content.

So I do not see how to follow Warnock's suggestion and,

regard, say Nietzsche—as of course he from time to time regarded himself
—not as propounding an unusual system of moral principles, but rather as
abandoning moral attitudes altogether, and as preaching 'beyond good and
evil' an ideal of conduct and character of an entirely different kind.

(p. 50)

Nietzsche's gestures this way are part of the consistent and
quite deliberate policy of exaggeration by which he tries to
startle us out of our grooves. To this end he uses every kind of
unexpected argument—metaphors, analogies, paradoxes of

every kind—to such effect that he has blinded his public to
the essential point—he is still arguing. Zarathustra descends
from the mountain. Much as he might admire Achilles, or
Attila, or Lucky Luciano, his methods are not theirs, nor are
his aims. As Warnock says, he *preaches*. His arguments
sometimes counter those of received morality—which suggests that they belong to the same subject anyway—but of
course sometimes they reinforce them. He attacks altruism by
exalting courage and honesty; if we did not honour those
virtues we could not follow him. He does not just tempt, he
claims to sting our consciences to follow him in the painful
duty of nonconformity. To abandon moral attitudes altogether
you would have to stop talking; to put your disregard for
other people consistently into practice, you would give up
formulating your ideals in their terms, as when you hypnotize
them, or silently throw your sword into the scales. A mentally
active person finds this very hard; even Callicles could not
resist an argument. Nietzsche's questions are those of the
moralist, because he stands at the moral point of view, asking
'how are we to live; what are the central things in life?' Are his
answers such as to exclude him? Warnock suggests evicting
from the moral sphere: 'such ideals as are openly destructive,
or damaging, or pointless, or insane'. Destructive of what? All
ideals involve destruction and damage to *something*; if only to
contrary life styles. Normally they promise compensation.
Savonarola offers us Heaven in return for a ravaged earth; the
Nazis set the glory of the master race against the destruction
of their servants. If we think what is offered has *some* value, we
can say they are bad moralists, who have got their values
wrong. If not, or *if no intelligible compensation is offered at all*,
then indeed moral argument stops. A revolutionary saying
'you must not ask what will happen after the Revolution'
seems to approach this point—but *if* he succeeds in showing
that revolution itself has a value, he will not reach it.
'Pointless' or 'insane' seem to mark the real frontier. What
stays outside is taboo, obsession, egoism, prejudice, etc. so
far as they are really mindless and uncommunicating. There
are also cases kept outside temporarily by our ignorance; until
we know what makes people tick we may not understand
what compensation they think there will be for the destruction

they propose. But where we can and do actually talk to people such things are rare, because the motives for comparing values intelligibly are so strong. Content and form are related. It is barely possible to communicate ideals with no element of altruism, or to make an ideal clear to oneself which is wholly unacceptable to everybody else. What is seriously held must in the end be intelligibly defended. It looks as if there is a link here between form and content, which would enable my point to be combined with Warnock's. But I cannot chase it now.

What, then, have we achieved if we say that there is a close link between morality and seriousness? Not, obviously, the elimination of humbug. Seriousness, too, is a notion which can very easily be made to stink, and I should guess that for some French writers it has collected the same sort of ambivalent response that *moral* has in English. So long as we are all hypocrites, all moral terms will be subject to this corruption. But I think *serious* has never gathered the suggestion which is so disastrous to *moral*, namely isolation. An unarguable, isolated taboo on a class of external acts, indefensible, behaviouristic, quite pure from all psychological or social justification, *must* involve humbug. Calling something serious implies that it is not isolated, that it is connected with other matters of undoubted importance. Argument is always in order. Humbug therefore is not endemic to the concept, which it is to moral in the sense named.

Suppose then we say that *the moral point of view is the one where we consider priorities, where we ask, 'what are the most serious, the central things in life?'* Then, when we oppose it to other points of view, say to the aesthetic or political, we are not comparing two separate and equal systems. We are stepping back from *all* the partial systems and looking at their relation to each other. If a musician must choose between the interests of his family and the interests of his work, what he has got is a moral problem, not because music conflicts with morality, but because finding the priority of music or anything else in the total scheme of things just is moral thinking. Music is one of the things which can constitute human good and harm, and it is among those things that we have to choose. Outside that range we cannot go anyway, which takes care of Hare's worry that people might want to invent entirely new values. And within it, the familiar considerations about other people's happiness, etc. are bound to play a central part while Homo Sapiens remains the intensely social, vulnerable, communicative creature that he genetically is. This should take care of Warnock's point about the content. See his excellent remark that 'we have no understanding of the evaluations of hypothetical Martians' (p. 67), simply because they *are* hypothetical; we could never be in this situation towards human beings, nor towards any other species, alien or otherwise, with whom we had actually to deal.

Just a word in conclusion. The main dispute in ethics these days lies between people who stress the *autonomy* of morals to avoid debasing them, and those who stress the *continuity of morals with other topics* in order to make them intelligible. What I have said here mainly supports the drive for intelligibility, but this is not because I think the other side unimportant. I believe a vigorous dialectic from both sides is called for, and now that we are getting out of the siding into which the intuitionists' odd notion of autonomy shunted us, we should be free to achieve it. The notion of autonomy itself is due for a shake-up. It was invented to free morality from excessive dependence on certain concepts which were becoming too powerful within it. It was not invented to cut it off from connection with *all* other topics, nor could it possibly do so. Kant, for instance, wanted to loosen the connection of morality with happiness, not so as to sterilize it in a vacuum, but so as to tighten its connection with rationality and freedom. Even Moore, whose practice was much better than his theory, wanted a looser connection with the sciences, but a closer one with the arts. Both of them, as much as Butler or Aristotle, set morality in the context of a quite definite view of what a human being is. Nietzsche, stressing in his turn the importance of freedom as against custom, uses the term for a different emphasis:[27]

In the end comes the sovereign individual, that resembles only himself, that has got loose from the morality of custom; the autonomous, super-moral individual (for *autonomous and moral are mutually exclusive terms*). . . .

But the effect of this is merely a new kind of psychological and metaphysical morality; we are to break the chains of custom in order to follow our own nature, which Nietzsche is ready to explain to us. If he were not, the whole thing would be vacuous. (As it is, the only vacuous phrase is 'resembles nobody but himself'.) This is a very powerful view today, and the surface revulsion I spoke of against the notion of human nature does not at all stop people reinforcing it with the ideas of Freud. I believe that some such preference is always understood, that the drive for autonomy in morals always means favouring one set of connections at the expense of another. The aim is never total isolation, which is clearly nonsense, but to resist certain particular systems (Freudian, Marxist, Christian, etc.) which want to take over morality, by pointing to important elements in life that they miss. This is entirely laudable. Beyond that, I think, there exists a less honourable, more masochistic idea that the more obscure solution is *always* the better in ethics; that the man who believes he has good grounds for the principles he acts on is a less noble character than the man who, whatever the arguments, is still gnawed for ever by agonized uncertainty. The idle scepticism behind this would be shown up soon enough today in any other branch of philosophy. There is always a space between the monster of complacency and the whirlpool of neurotic dither, and our dialectic will somehow have to find it.

8 THE GAME GAME

Some people talk about football as if it were life and death itself, but it is much more serious than that.

        (Bill Shankly, manager of Liverpool Football Club)

Some time ago, an Innocent Bystander, after glancing through a copy of *Mind*, asked me, 'Why do philosophers talk so much about games? Do they play them a lot or something?'

Well, why do they? Broadly, because they are often discussing situations where there are rules, but where we are not sure why the rules have to be obeyed. Treating them as Rules of a Game fends off this problem for the time. And should it turn out that the reasons for playing games are in fact perfectly simple, it might even solve it completely. This hope shines through numerous discussions. I shall deal here with one of the simplest; namely Hare's on *The Promising Game*,[1] which suggested that our duty to keep promises was simply part of the game or institution of promising, and that if we decided not to play that game, the duty would vanish. That suggestion is the starting-point of this paper. It has made me ask, all right, what sort of need is the need to obey the rules of games? Why start? Why not cheat? What is the sanction? And again, how would things go if we decided tomorrow *not* to play the Promising game, or the Marriage Game or the Property Game? What is gained by calling them games? What, in fact, *is* a game?

Problems about definition and generality come up here. Can such general questions be asked at all? They come up with special force, because of two diverging elements in the philosophic talk of games. On my right, apparently, games are things we can say very little about; on my left, they are things we can talk of boldly. On my right, that is, Wittgenstein used 'game' as the prime example of a word which we

cannot define by finding a single feature common to all its
instances: they are linked only by a meandering string of
family resemblances. He is attacking the idea of a fixed, given
essence which language seeks out and definition can capture.
There is, he says, no underlying unity; all that games have in
common is that they are games. On my left we have a number
of philosophers (including Wittgenstein himself) who suggest
that we do have a firm grasp of the underlying unity, by using
the word in metaphorical phrases like 'language game'. Now
metaphor is hardly possible where we don't have a pretty
clear, positive idea of the root notion. To give a parallel, when
the early Church spoke of Christ as the Light of the World,
the metaphor succeeded because people knew very well what
lights have in common, namely a certain relation to the things
and people lit—although if you think about the differences
between lights you might find they varied as much in detail as
games do. Or again, to pick up the point about family
resemblances, it is possible to use the term BORGIA as a
metaphor because we take the Borgias to have something in
common apart from being linked by their family resemblances. If I say 'for goodness sake don't go to supper with
him: he's a sort of a Borgia', my metaphor works, but if I
substitute Jones or any other surname where we do know only
a string of family resemblances, it won't work. In the same
way, philosohers must, I think, know what the underlying
unity linking things called 'games' is if their constant use of
this metaphor is to be justified. When Wittgenstein considered the problem of finding 'one thing in common' between
all the various games, he noted the shifting network of surface
similarities, and said:

I can think of no better expression to characterize these similarities than
'family resemblances'; for the various resemblances between members of a
family, build, features, colour of eyes, gait, temperament, etc., etc. overlap
and criss-cross in the same way—And I shall say, 'games' form a family.
(*Philosophical Investigations*, 67, cf. *Blue Book* p. 17–18)

But to form a family is quite a different thing from having a
family resemblance. Elliots need not have the Elliot coun-

tenance at all; they may be quite untypical, and plausible-looking Tichborne Claimants need not be Tichbornes. A family is a functional group with a concentric structure, a centre, and well-understood rules governing the claims of outlying members. This difference becomes still clearer with Wittgenstein's next simile of the thread:

And we extend our concept (of number) as in spinning a thread we twist fibre on fibre. And the strength of the thread does not reside in the fact that some one fibre runs through its whole length, but in the overlapping of many fibres.

(*Philosophical Investigations*, 67)

But threads must end somewhere; how do we know when to cut them off? This argument proves too much. As Kovesi remarks:

I do not see any foundation for a claim that we call both football and chess 'games' because football is played with a ball, and so is tennis, while tennis is played by two people, and so is chess. Not only is this insufficient to explain that connection between football and chess which makes both of them games, but this way we could connect everything to everything else. We could turn off at a tangent at every similarity and what we would get in the end would not be a rope but a mesh. Balls, cannonballs, were used to bombard cities, and duelling is a matter for two people. What we need in order to understand the notion of a game or the notion of murder is what I call the formal element. This is what enables us to follow a rule.

(*Moral Notions*, p. 22)

If we could not follow the rule, we would never know where to draw the line. But this is just the kind of concept where drawing the line is most crucial. Is it oppression? Is it exploitation? Is it murder? This type of question is what brings 'common elements' and 'underlying unities' into the limelight. We need them. '*Is it a game?*' asks the anxious mother listening to the yells upstairs, the eager anthropologist watching the feathered figures round the fire, the hopeful child or dog watching the surveyors place their chains, the puzzled reader of *Games People Play*. They can all *use* the concept, because it does have some principle of unity, because it is not infinitely elastic. They all take their stand, not on the same point, but on the same small island of meaning—a firm island with a definite shape. By contrast, anyone asking today, 'Is it a work of art?' may simply find himself floundering over ankles in water, because that island has been shovelled off in all directions into the sea, in a set of deliberate attempts to extend it for propaganda purposes. 'Don't think, but look!' says Wittgenstein. But we need to think in order to know what to look for.

I am not now going to take on the whole enormous subject of Wittgenstein's general attack on generality, nor even ask his reasons for speaking of a 'craving for generality' as something morbid, when one does not so speak of a craving for fragmentation. I do not think that he meant, what many philosophers have assumed, that there are *no* limits to the conventions human language might adopt; that in principle anything goes. But I shall investigate only this single concept of a game. I want to look at the sense in which we *do* know what is in common between games, the sense in which there is an underlying unity. I hope both that this may be a helpful example when we wonder about other examples of seeing something in common, and that the concept itself may be a more important one than it seems, and may cast some light on the serious.

What, then is meant by such moves as calling promising a 'game'? I shall follow up R. M. Hare's case of the Promising Game because I think it is a typical, though unusually clear, example of the suggestion that anything might go. Hare was answering John Searle's suggestion that the duty of keeping promises might simply follow from the fact of having made them. Hare replied 'that depends on whether you have agreed to play the Promising game or not'. He wanted, that is, to treat promising as one of the many dispensable games or institutions which people could adopt or not as they chose. Only our narrow-mindedness, said Hare, made us assume that promising or any other institution is particularly basic; people with different views might choose different ones, just as they might prefer poker to bezique.

Obviously, the game parallel is very useful to Hare here, because it makes it easy to treat promising as optional. Of course, we think, a game is a self-contained system, an enclave which can be dropped without upsetting the surrounding scenery, an activity discontinuous with the life around it. It wouldn't matter whether we played baseball or cricket, poker or scrabble: it wouldn't matter if we invented a new game or didn't play any of them at all. That, we reflect, is part of the meaning of game. We really seem to have that rare thing, so precious to Hare, a pure decision without reasons. Games, in fact never matter.

Now this is a distinctly queer account of promising. First, if there were no promising, could there be games? As many of us have found, consenting to play, say, cricket, usually turns out to have involved promising not to go to sleep while fielding deep, or stomp off in a fury if one is bowled, etc. In this way, rejecting the 'promising game' might make all other games and institutions impossible as well. (Other examples given are marriage and property, which do involve promising, and speech, which seems involved in the whole lot.) We may be no better off than those who derived the duty of keeping promises from the Social Contract—no promising; no contract, and in the same way, no promising, no game.

Second and converging, Hare doesn't say anything about what the promiseless world would be like. Philosophers are rather prone to throw out claims like 'I can imagine a tribe which . . .' without going to the trouble of actually doing it. I suspect this has happened here from certain of Hare's casual remarks, e.g.., 'Suppose that nobody thought that one ought to keep promises. It would then be impossible to make a promise; the word 'promise' would become a mere noise, except . . . for anthropologists.' (p. 124.)

When nobody keeps promises anymore, how will there be any anthropologists? Who is paying them? What does he use for money? (Note the wording on a pound note.) What ship did they travel out on? How will they publish? Who will believe them? This is no more understandable than the equally inspiring converse suggestion made by Phillips and Mounce, who say, 'Let us consider a people who have the practice of promise-keeping, *and let us suppose that this is their sole moral practice*' (*Moral Practices* p. 10, my italics). Thus a botanist might ask us to consider a plant which has fruit, and to suppose that is all it has—no roots, stem, leaves or flower.

What follows? Until you tell us more, anything you please. Nietzsche, no great enthusiast for moral dogmatism, gave a better account of the position of promising at the head of his essay on 'Guilt, Bad Conscience and the Like':

The breeding of an animal that *can promise*—is not this just that very paradox of a task which nature has set itself with regard to man? Is not this the very problem of man? . . . At the end of this colossal process . . . we find . . . the man of the personal, long and independent will, *competent to promise.*
(*Genealogy of Morals*, Essay 2, Section 1)

Taking this with the importance given to commitment in existentialist thinking, we can see that not everyone who treats the morality of custom lightly thinks that promising is part of it.

Perhaps then, promising is not very like a game. It may be more like the institution of playing games in general, if by chance there is such a thing. In fact, it is not *an* institution at all; it is a condition of having institutions. And this point would have been much more obvious, were it not for the plausible parallel of the game.

I do not want here to pursue the question about the basis of promising so much as to investigate the notion of games as closed systems. This, I suggested, means that they are discontinuous with the life around them. That seems to be how the term is used in mathematics; the theory of games deals with a certain set of closed systems. In this sense, no question arises about the reasons or motives for playing; there is no suggestion of playfulness or jollity in the ordinary sense. But of course, when you bring the term into moral philosophy and apply it to people's *actual* activities, the reasons and motives begin to matter. Any actual activity has motives, and it won't be a closed system, optional and removable, unless the motives are of a special kind. They must not be very strong, or it will begin to matter whether we play or not; they must not be very specific, or it will begin to matter *which* game we play. If they are strong or specific, the system will not be self-contained.

I want to suggest that some quite complex points about

motives and reasons for playing are part of the ordinary meaning of game; that the philosopher's use to denote simply a closed system (abstracting from these) is most misleading. Both Manser and Khatchadourian[2] have brought this up, and so far as they go I agree with them. But each of them stresses just one point about games (Khatchadourian pleasure, Manser the separation from common life) and not even the two together are enough to distinguish games from the surrounding scenery. For instance, both these points apply also to art, telly-watching, wine-fancying or the miser's delight in his gold, and none of these are games. We know a lot more about games than this, and there is nothing to be said for affecting ignorance.

I should like to examine the concept further, and see how complete the separation of games from common life is.

First, then I want to say that even *actual* games, normally classed as such, do not keep themselves to themselves in this way but flow over in a perfectly recognized way into the rest of life. Secondly, I want to mention some extended, but still perfectly proper, uses of 'game' and related concepts, like 'playing'. These uses may be metaphorical, but they are quite natural and familiar and tell us a lot about why people play. If Hare's notion of the Promising Game has a place it is among these extended uses, so they are highly relevant. Until we understand the reasons for playing, I do not think we understand the bindingness of the rules.

I turn, then, first to actual existing games, called so without metaphor. How far is it true that they are closed systems, discontinuous with the rest of life?

In a simple way, this looks obvious; in fact it looks like *the* characteristic point about a game. You buy little books of the rules for a given game, and they will tell you how to start and stop playing, but not how to fit these procedures into the rest of your life. What happens in a game can be contrasted with what happens in (as we say)'real' life, and a person taking his game animosity too strongly may be checked with the reminder, 'Relax man, calm down, remember it's only a game.' This is true where the motives for playing are weak and largely negative, which they often are: we want the simple rewards of play as a change from the strains of serious life.

But often there are positive motives. If you say to a grand-master, 'Calm down, chess is only a game' your point will be obscure. Chess is the business of his life; he may have no other. This may also be true of children. Similarly when Rangers play Celtic, not only may people get killed, but the event is central to the lives of many people present. (I have seen a press report of someone interviewing boys from the Gorbals, who asked them, 'Which is the best of these four things: Drink, Sex, Fighting and Celtic?' and got the answer, 'Celtic every time.') Should we say that this concern attached to a game is accidental; it just happens to have become hitched on to it? But Russian Roulette is a game, and death is an essential part of it, and the same insistence on real danger shows up in many forms of gambling ('it isn't poker if you play for love') and indeed of cheating.

In the case of football or chess, to treat the traditional concern as accidental would mean that it could just as well be attached to something else; that the pattern of life surround-ing them demands *some* game, but is quite indifferent what game it is. Well then, we will try substituting halma for chess and lawn tennis for football. Will there be any difficulties? There will. These rituals *will not be suitable forms for the conflicts they are designed to ritualize*. Halma cannot stand in for chess because it is too simple; were the change imposed by law, the result would be an inconceivable complication of the rules of halma. Lawn tennis will not do instead of football for some quite interesting reasons. It is not a team game; it involves no physical contact and does not make the players dirty. More-over there are rackets, which, if used in the spirit of football, might kill people. Any attempt to substitute it would result, either in changing lawn tennis past recognition, or (more likely) in the public's abandoning tennis and inventing instead some much more primitive ritualized contest of the kind from which football originally sprang.

These games are continuous with the life around them, and their selection is not at all optional or arbitrary. The Rule Book is misleading; or rather, it misleads those few unhappy people who expect to see the whole truth about anything written down in a book. Books take obvious points for granted. For instance, the book does not mention spectators, nor the reasons for playing and the kind and degree of friendliness called for between players: nor does it mention the choice of teams and opponents, but every game makes quite complicated demands here. Nor does it mention how you give up playing, but that doesn't show there are no proper or improper ways of doing it. (Anyone giving up chess in Russia or football in Glasgow would soon find out about that.) It is just these unwritten parts of a game which are distorted when games are played in schools under compulsion. Compulsion can kill the game stone dead, which shows how much they matter.

Games, in fact, spring from the life around them, because games are, among other things, *ritualized conflict*, and the type of ritual is by no means arbitrary, but must fit the kind of conflict which is already going forward. Such ritual proceedings are not at all an optional extra, a froth on human life, peculiar to advanced and leisurely cultures. They are extremely widespread, if not universal, throughout the human race, and are also found in a wide variety of animals. The lower the animal, the more standardized the proceedings; higher mammals and particularly primates have a much richer repertoire. But throughout the animal kingdom quite elaborate rituals surround a fight, as well as other social occasions, entirely discrediting the traditional notion of formless and uncontrolled savagery in Nature.

Actual games, then, are not closed systems in the sense of being arbitrary, optional and discontinuous with the life around them. They are systems, but not closed ones. What about metaphorical games?

Moralists have used the metaphor of a game rather widely, which is not surprising since it is widely used in common life ('So that's your game?', 'The game's up', 'Playing a waiting game', 'a deep game', etc.) I want to look at some of these uses, along with those of related ideas like 'sport' and 'play', so as to throw some light on what we are doing when we say that something is or is not a game.

One notable and familiar use is the one in which the sour fatalist calls All Life a Game, or something like it, in the sense that it is futile, pointless or absurd. Thus, in Hardy: 'The President of the Immortals had ended his sport with Tess'. Or

Gloucester in *King Lear* 'As flies to wanton boys are we to the Gods. They kill us for their sport." Or Omar Khayyam:

> Tis all a chequer-board of Nights and Days
> Where Destiny with men for pieces plays.
> Hither and thither moves, and mates, and slays,
> And one by one back in the closet lays.

Now, this does come close to the notion of a closed and arbitrary system. But then it is a use you cannot rest in if you think beyond your first hasty comment, because games are not arbitrary in this way. Someone plays them; he has a purpose in playing whether the pawns understand it or not. Thus Hardy would have done better not to turn our attention from Tess to the President of the Immortals, a subject on which he is much less convincing. This use of the concept may be meant in the first place to stress the arbitrariness and disconnection of our life, but if we put any weight on it, it will do something quite different and give it a context; pointing to a purpose beyond our ordinary aims and possibly much more important than them. (Compare the curiosity about Godot roused by *Waiting for Godot*).

There are other ways in which the notion of games can be used to enforce seriousness. Even without the thought of a divine player or spectator, the figure is common in Stoic morality. Epictetus, for instance, uses it when he finds a difficulty in explaining his concept of seriousness. He indicates by it that he wants us to be detached from ordinary life so far as to despise its rewards, but does not want us to drop back with a sigh of relief into the Cynic's barrel or the Epicurean's garden seat, to be strenuous yet not anxious, committed yet free. Again, to our surprise, we find that very serious character Plato telling us that 'human affairs are not worth much serious attention' (Laws 803b), but that since we have unfortunately got to consider them, the only important question is, what sort of play are we to spend our time on? What life is really about, Plato explains, is playing to amuse God. God is our central business and also our most satisfying play. A modern writer who is still more interested in such motives, and who seems to me to throw a lot of light on them is Jan Huizinga in his book *Homo Ludens*. Huizinga's point is that play is an essential element in all highly regarded human activities, and may in some sense be called the basis of all of them. Stylized patterns akin to play are found in the rituals of religion, in lawsuits and court ceremonial, in the formal feuds of politics, in family life and in the play of lovers, in war, and above all in art. All these activities have rules which matter greatly and yet do not really matter at all, in much the same paradoxical manner as the rules of a game. None of them would be as they are without the taste for certain definite kinds of *ritualized conflict*.

It does not follow that this taste is perverted or frivolous. It is a mistake to think that what is regulated must be trivial, that the needs involved must be weak or they would be stronger than the rule. The restraining rules are not something foreign to the needs or emotions involved, they are simply the shape which the desired activity takes. The chess player's desire is not a desire for general abstract intellectual activity, curbed and frustrated by a particular set of rules. It is a desire for a particular kind of intellectual activity, whose channel is the rules of chess. Similarly, human love is not a general need, curbed and frustrated by the particular forms offered to it. It is a need for a specific kind of relation—say a permanent one—with a particular person, and for this purpose only some kinds of behaviour will do. The football player similarly does not just want to rush about kicking things. He wants to do so in a special context of ordered competition with companions: he needs to know what sort of response he will get and who has won. Similarly, as Huizinga points out, rituals like court ceremonial are not arbitrary restrictions clogging personal intercourse. In their origin, when courts meant something, they were forms, and suitable forms, by which subjects could express their loyalty and kings their kingliness. Forms can die, but formality is not deadness. Huizinga's remarks stress the value of play in human life, the profound and complex need there is for it. Because this need is complex, the things which satisfy it will not share any obvious simple characteristic, like being painted green, but because it is strong and universal, they will share structural charac-

teristics which are easily recognised, not only by others of
their own species but even by outsiders. (This successful
signalling can be studied for instance in the dealings of people
with dogs, and in the pleasing situation where zoo visitors,
observing the animals, are themselves observed by keepers
and ethologists.)[3] Where a need is shared, we know what
marks to look for. The need for play is subtle and complex.
We do not fully understand it. Huizinga exalts play by
stressing the links between this need and what are generally
supposed to be man's most important activities. Eric Berne,
on the other hand, points out, in *Games People Play*, its strength
and thereby something rather more sinister about it, namely
its obsessiveness, the way in which a taste for play can get the
better of us, entangling us and frustrating our other needs.
But both points of course suggest that the need is no trivial
one, and both equally, if accepted, tell against the suggestion
that games as such do not matter.

Berne's point converges with Huizinga's. Play is found
pervading our most important concerns; play insists on being
taken seriously. We need it. Can we say why? I think
Huizinga is perfectly right to connect this issue with the
equally mysterious question of the purpose or value of art.
Whatever that purpose or purposes may be, art does share
with play the paradoxical property of being somehow set
aside from the prodding practical purposes of life, and yet
asserting at times a mysterious right to preodominate over
them. If one says that art cannot affect life, one is liable to be
brought up by the thought of someone who has jumped off the
Clapham omnibus and gone away to devote his life to it, or by
the reflection that nobody's life will be quite the same again
after he has read the *Agamemnon* of Aeschylus properly. Apart
from that, the activities used in art—singing, dancing, drawing etc.—do not belong to a select minority, they are all
prominent in the play of children, and a taste for them can be
detected in young apes as well. One could look here towards
the peculiar biological characteristic of man called Neoteny,
that is, the extension of infantile characteristics into adult life.[4]
This is a device by which a species often exploits a possibility
already present in its genetic make-up, but previously limited
to an early phase, by prolonging that phase. People resemble

baby apes, and even embryo apes, much more strongly than they resemble adult apes, on a number of points of physical development, but of course most notably in their large and quick-growing brain. An ape or monkey brain completes its grown in 6–12 months from birth; a human brain goes on growing for about 23 years. And a related pattern can be seen in the development of behaviour. Playing at all is behaviour confined to relatively intelligent, active, big-brained, non-specialist animals, and where it occurs, it occurs mostly in the young. Now the free, enquiring use of the intellect belongs originally in this context of play. Nearly all the experiments on primate learning and intelligence are done with ape babies and children; once an ape is adult he gets above such things, loses interest and refuses to co-operate—he may even turn nasty. But in man, it is just this use of the intellect which is prolonged into adult life. Does it carry play patterns with it? Is the taste for problem-solving, for ritual, for constantly formalizing disputes and taking sides a relic of the matrix within which exploratory thought emerged? And is the aesthetic approach another? (Apes show the rudiments of dance forms, continuing even into adult life, and have in childhood a pronounced taste for painting.)[5] This seems to me a real and perplexing issue. Perhaps a *mature* pattern of behaviour, suitable for a creature possessing a mature human brain, is something that has not yet been evolved. That might explain more than one of our difficulties.

I return now to Hare's suggestion about the Promising Game. My point in surveying the extended uses of game has been to draw the meanings that emerge from it when you use it metaphorically. Metaphor, I suggested, is an epidiascope projecting enlarged images of a word's meaning; turn the word round and you get different pictures, but where we don't grasp an underlying unity we can get no metaphor at all, and where the meaning isn't what we hope, the metaphor will fail. Now if anyone thinks that all the people I have quoted fail in their metaphors—that they are simply misusing 'game' and 'play', he will of course reject my argument. My own impression about this is that Plato and Huizinga *are* somewhat paradoxical; they do make a rather startling use of the word 'play' but justify it by the clearness and fertility of their point; they make us see after a moment's thought that *play* might really not be a bad word for the things they apply it to, and they thereby throw a new light on the notion of seriousness. Berne and the Stoics on the other hand don't seem to me to use the word *game* surprisingly at all, only to extend and enlarge perfectly normal uses along the lines already laid down. The Stoic notion about playing the game has been good common morality down to our own day, and until the public schools got hold of it there was nothing ridiculous about it at all. And what Berne says about chronic quarrelling or scenes of remorse might well occur to any experienced bystander; calling these a game is hardly a metaphor, it is one in a vigorous series of extremely common uses—he's taken up the con game, honesty's his game at present, daughters of the game. These uses are hardly more metaphorical than 'seeing' or 'grasping' a point in argument. There is no more literal phrase available. And as all these uses stress in the end the importance of games, not-mattering cannot be the central point about them. But there is of course a sense in which games do not matter, in which they are considered as cut off from other activities, and there would be nothing to stop Hare making successful use of the concept from this angle—it is the beauty of a rich concept like this that you *can* get a lot of metaphors out of it. Has he done so?

If we examine that sense, we are struck at once by its failure to fit Hare's point. Games, for instance, are shut off from *each other*, far more sharply than they are shut off from the rest of life—you cannot play cricket and football at the same time. But these metaphorical games are closely interwoven. Marriage cannot be played without other games like promising, and can generate an indefinite number of further games, all in definite relations to it. A married, religious, liberal, promise-keeping physicist plays his five games, not only simultaneously but in a pretty closely-ordered structure because—a point which seems to have been overlooked—he has only got one life to live, and he needs to make sense of it. Therefore he has to try all the time to fit them together and work out his priorities. Of course he will often fail and get confused, which is what makes the suggestion of separating them seem plausible. *But if he gave up the attempt entirely, he would*

be making it his policy to let his personality disintegrate. This cannot
be treated as an optional further game, because it is negative
and rule-less; moreover, it means losing the capacity for any
further human enterprise whatsoever. To press the point, has
this man now one game or five games? And could these games
possibly fail to involve others—teacher, truth-teller, pupil,
citizen, property-owner, colleague, friend, Jew, customer—
you name it? And the involvement is deep. This man's
marriage will be a *different kind of marriage* from that of a man
without religion, and his religion a different kind of religion
from that of a man with no knowledge of science. This is not
just an external relation, like that between a grandmaster's
chess and the football he may play to keep in training. It is
more like that between marriage and parenthood, or between
my political views and and my view of history. They *must* be
congruent to work at all, and where they change they must
change together. Certainly we often fail to relate aspects of
our lives; we become dishonest, hypocritical and confused.
But these are the names of faults, not of the norm. Where we
do this (to repeat the obvious) we pay for it in confusion of
life, in ineffectiveness and disintegration of the personality.
*We do not actually have the option of splitting ourselves into a viable
batch of coral polyps.* And it is just in the necessary business of
relating these aspects that most of our moral problems arise,
so that a philosopher who rules that nothing can be said about
it has shown his uselessness pretty thoroughly. Thus the *game*
metaphor dissolves in confusion.

We see this again if we try to imagine the transaction of
'stopping playing'. Unless we can point to some kind of
possible world without (say), promising, calling it 'just an
institution' will be rather like calling the world we actually
live in 'just a dream.' (It might have a meaning, but not for
us.) Hare describes the *invention* of promising as taking place
among a people whose language is already so far advanced in
abstraction as to include the word 'obligation' in its modern
general sense (a sense which has only emerged in European
thought in the last two centuries), and describes it as consisting in linking that idea with a speech ritual. But how did they
get that far without any promising? Is their language supposed to have contained no performative words before? If it

did, are they supposed not to have minded when people using
them then went on to act as if they had not done so? The
resulting confusion and difficulty must be at least as great as
that where people constantly tell lies; is the objection to *that*
supposed to be also an optional institution? This need is at
least as old as the need for speech itself; it is the first condition
of co-operation. Animals like wolves have other ways of
holding a dialogue like, 'I'll go round and drive the antelope
into the valley'. 'Right, I'll wait for them under this tree.'
Men, developing speech, could not fail to use it for this very
important purpose. How could it *not matter*, not be objected to,
if one of the speakers then went off to sleep instead? How
could this fail to be a concern for morality as it develops?

To give some positive evidence—Ruth Benedict, emphasiz-
ing the very wide variations there can be in human habits,
remarks that there are 'very few traits that are universal or
near-universal in human society. There are several that are
well known. Of these everyone agrees on . . . the exogamous
restrictions upon marriage.' But marriage after all involves
promising. Actually, the most hopeful example I know of an
almost non-promising society is Ruth Benedict's Dobu, who
she says, 'put a premium on ill-will and treachery and made
of them the recognized virtues of their society'. '*Behind a show
of friendship, behind the evidences of co-operation*, in every field of
life, the Dobu believes he has only treachery.'[6] But (as the
words I have italicized make clear) this happy state of affairs
is, of course, parasitical on promising. The show of friendship, the evidences of co-operation, must be there and must
still largely be believed in, for treachery to flourish. 'Only
treachery' has to be a gross exaggeration, like 'a world
consisting only of exceptions'. That Dobu culture-hero, the
successful con-man, is doomed to defeat himself unless he
remembers this. As one of them sadly says: 'I cannot [bilk
creditors] for too long, or my exchanges will never be trusted
by anyone again. I am honest in the final issue.' In effect, both
he and the Machiavellian politician mentioned by Hare are
small-time operators tinkering within an established pattern,
not Nietzschean supermen who have invented something
quite different. They differ from ordinary promisers only in
the relative importance they give to the obligation of promising

as against other motives. On top of this the Dobu is of course operating at a very primitive level, in a shame-culture which could make nothing of Hare's abstract notion of 'obligation', and the Machiavellian politician may be doing that too. But whatever sense they do give to obligation, promising has to carry it.

Thus it is hard to see what a promiseless society would be like, and the burden of argument seems to lie on those who claim the thing makes sense. If it does not, it is misleading to call promising, or any other very general moral form, a game or an institution, assimilating it to particular local forms like Freemasonry or driving on the left of the road. What misleads us here is, of course, that *a* game, and *an* institution, are terms used for systems of varying sizes, often for concentric ones, such as speech, promising and trial by jury, and Hare has assumed that, because you can readily change the smallest example of each, you can change all the others in the same way. Thus your picking up a rock proves that you could pick up the Bass Rock, and your taking off your coat and jacket proves you can take off your skin as well. Speech is not really an institution at all, nor is sex, nor is playing games, nor walking upright, nor weeping nor laughing, nor loving one's children, nor marriage, nor property, nor promising, though the forms all these things take in different societies will of course be so. The word 'institution' would be best saved for things which were once instituted and could at a pinch be disinstituted again without taking the entire human race with them.

So much for the philosopher's misuse of this particular concept, *game*. I return to the wider point about definition, of which I have suggested this case is an instance—the need to look for 'underlying unities'.

Why does this matter? Because, as I have suggested a great number of the concepts that actually do the work in moral discussion today are general ones which are in the same sort of trouble as 'game'. Since they do a lot of work we *must* try to define them and look for underlying unities (here they are unlike 'family resemblance', an idle concept if ever there was one) and yet we shall certainly not be able to give a single plain litmus-paper test for them because their point is structural, and not at all like that of colour-words. Such concepts are—exploitation, oppression, sanity, disease, pollution, fulfilment, justice, freedom, art form, escapism, obscurity, sexual, serious, normal. Suppose we took Wittgenstein's line about one of these—suppose we said for instance that the only thing all cases of exploitation had in common was that they were cases of exploitation—should we be better off or worse when we have to decide whether something is a case of exploitation or not, than we are when we constantly look for an underlying unity? As things are we may indeed employ a number of different marks, but only on the assumption that they have some sort of connection with one another and are aspects of an underlying structure. Otherwise the concept falls to pieces, as indeed, the concept of art has already done. We do assume a unity in such concepts, and we are not silly to do so, because they all deal with human needs, which certainly do have a structure. Man is an animal given to exploitation, and he is also a game-playing animal. The business of moral philosophy starts with the analysis of such concepts. If all we had to do in moral philosophy was to wait for people to pronounce moral judgements like 'x is good', life might perhaps be simpler, but far less interesting. And we would certainly be members of a so far unknown species, not Homo sapiens.

9 THE NOTION OF INSTINCT

Granted that there are inherited tendencies affecting human behaviour, what terms should we use to describe them? The three words which most naturally come to mind are drive, program and instinct. All three have their separate problems. *Drive* is a dynamic word, a word about forces. It answers the question 'why is this done *at this intensity*?' *Program* is a communication word, a term concerned with information 'coded' in the genes. It answers the question, 'why is *this* done, rather than something else?' These two technical models are very different. Both are useful; both need watching. *Instinct*, on the other hand is a much older, broader, less technical word, with a rich crust of associations, some of them misleading. Many people like to throw out all such words, crying with B. F. Skinner that 'the vernacular is clumsy and obese'.[1] They want clean equipment. This wish is what has made drive and programme so popular. But to take this line you have to be sure that you have grasped the underlying problem. New words only help where the thought has been cleared up. Confusions in traditional conceptual schemes usually reflect some difficulty in the subject-matter; they are not just surface dirt. Whatever new scheme we propose will have *some* relation to the traditional one, and that connection had better be clear and explicit.

In the teeth of current fashion, I am inclined to think that *instinct* will prove in the end the most generally useful of these three terms, just because it does combine the dynamic with the communicative model. It originally meant a voice within —an instigator—which is conceived both as a source of information on what to do, and as a force impelling us to do it. And it is likely that these ideas are in fact connected. Moreover, this word has been effectively cleaned up in the last few decades by zoologists; its use for animals is now reasonably clear. Provided that we understand it properly and exploit its subtleties, we can safely use it of people. Homo sapiens is not so monstrously different from other species as to make comparison impossible. As the facts of evolution might make us expect, his distinctness is an intelligible one. 'Animals' vary immensely, but the continuity amongst them is a necessary key to all variety.

The trouble with this notion of instincts as voices used to be that people took it literally and added an imaginary speaker —the species, the life-force, evolution, nature, God. But we need no such entity. (Least of all do we need the latest and most astonishing recruit to their number, the personified gene.) Information here means simply a formula, a specification. And evidently all organisms do develop in accordance with such an internal formula, as well as in response to their environment. There is nothing extravagant or anti-empirical about this. Empiricism does not demand that we use always the simplest conceptual scheme: schemes must be effective as well as simple. Nor does it call on us to reject the information model in advance, *a priori*, on the ground that all knowledge is derived from experience. Certainly nobody can smuggle into the world 'innate ideas' in the sense of explicit propositions, consciously known. Nobody is born knowing that Edinburgh is to the north of London. None the less, creatures of the most varied species are born equipped to react selectively, without conditioning, to very complex and improbable stimuli, and this is information 'coded' in the genes. Among animal examples, we might mention cuckoos, who commit several strenuous murders, quite uninstructed, the moment they get out of the egg, and thereafter go through with the whole arduous and unlikely business of being cuckoos, including finding cuckoo-food, migrating to particular places in Africa and finding other cuckoos to mate with, quite regardless of the intense and unbroken conditioning campaign which is trying to turn them into reed-warblers or hedge-sparrows. Of course they do not know *that* they are cuckoos, but they know *how* to be.[2] Among human examples, a good case is the baby's early response to the pattern of a smile. It can recognize smiles (either in a drawing or on a face) at the age of a few weeks, when it is quite incapable of recognizing other patterns, and it responds with an answering smile. Again, there is the tendency to babble and imitate which makes it capable of speech. How shall we describe such powers? Chomsky has teased empiricists by giving the name 'innate ideas' to the forms on which speech develops. His challenge is real, and it still holds whether or not we accept his detailed views about language. The tendency to talk, and to talk in specific ways, sometimes contrary to conditioning, is real. No doubt, however, the word 'idea' is not now a very suitable term to express it. Descartes (Chomsky's source) did use the term *innate ideas* to mean tendencies or capacities,[3] though he confused things by sometimes talking as if necessary truths came along with them. Locke took Descartes to be saying that fully formed thoughts were innate, and campaigned against this exaggeration, a campaign which empiricists have, somewhat absent-mindedly, continued ever since. Of course Descartes' exaggeration is wrong. But the specific, inborn tendencies to certain highly improbable ways of acting and feeling are real. The difficulty is just to disentangle them from acquired elements, and to describe them clearly.

Three main questions, then, arise:

1. How specific are such tendencies?
2. How are they distinguished from each other? How individuated or counted?
3. What is the relation between them? Should they be conceived as distinct atoms or as part of a given structure?

Question 1 about specificity is extremely important, because the main objection to applying such notions as 'instinct' to man at all is the belief that instincts are by definition highly specific, 'closed' programmes like those often found in insects for such things as hive-building and honey-dances. But, even at the insect level, not all instincts are like this. No creature that was merely a mechanical toy could survive a day. The closed programmes have to be supplemented by open ones with slots for facts about the world. Thus, bees and wasps learn the position of their hive and return to it by complex landmarks; they also learn to recognize a danger. This is the aspect of instinctive life on which behaviourists

have concentrated. It is not, however, an absence of programme, as they have sometimes thought, but a more complex sort of program, including a gap for an unknown
quantity—but one of a suitable kind. Beyond this, however,
even insects are capable of exploratory behaviour. They *search*,
and in searching they attend selectively to the kind of things
they will need to find.

In going up the evolutionary scale, we find a quite steady
increase in the openness of programs. We do not have to
wait for man for this to begin. The long fixed sequences are
progressively broken up to allow for more various methods.
Exploratory behaviour becomes more and more important.
Needs become more general. Social interaction gets richer as
the range of possible emotions is widened, and the expression
of them proliferates through the use of symbols. More and
more variation is possible. Yet it has limits; the details must
still fit the basic structure. Ernst Mayr argues very interestingly that the evolutionary choice between an open and closed
program tends to be settled on the principle that *exploration*
must be free and open, but *communication* needs some fixed
points.[4] Signals must be designed to get across, and since an
infant must give and receive emotional messages before it
can design and impose a private system, it has to be equipped
from the start with the basic set. This set therefore has to be
innate, and it is so in our own as well as other species. Even
speech is not altogether an exception to this rule but a
specialized example of it. Speech must be *vocal*; there is no
option about that. So babies naturally babble, attend to talk,
and respond very early to the tones, as well as imitating the
words, of those around them. For the deaf and dumb,
artificial substitutes are invented, but their artificiality is a
real handicap.

It is very interesting too that even in human life some larger
examples of relatively closed instinctive patterns are found in
this area. Culture can often prevent the expression of
emotion, but if expression is allowed at all, its natural forms
are very resistant to culture. We can have great trouble in
controlling them, and when we fail, quite long sequences of
behaviour can emerge which are not culturally acceptable,
which the person concerned may never have seen in his life,

and which are to a startling extent the same in everyone. (This indeed is one of the alarming things about them: they are impersonal and do not seem clearly related to an individual character.) A fit of hysterics or fury or panic fear is not much more flexible than the nest-building of the weaver-bird.

Still, in human conduct our main interest must obviously be, not in such detailed behaviour-patterns but in the large, inclusive patterns of motive like fear, sex, curiosity, play, the care of the young, each comprising many strands. And we already have good reason to be interested in these quite apart from wanting to understand the evolutionary context. For the most urgent practical purposes, as well as for theoretical purposes, we often need to interpret and classify motives. Moreover, in choosing our course of action we must often ask, first, what major need does this particular activity serve? And then, how important is that need? What is its place in the general structure of human needs? Which is the more weighty of two competing elements in life? What will be the price to be paid—in health, in emotion, in creativity—if we sacrifice this activity to that? Social conditioning cannot answer these questions. We are all capable of being dissatisfied with our conditioning. Habit is just one element in life among others, and our need to form habits is just one of our needs. Educators and parents have often tried to condition their young into total order, chastity, silence, obedience and the like without success. Substitute activities—symbols—can often be accepted, but only within limits, and they still need to be understood. Besides, even where a pattern is successfully imposed, questions can still arise about the bargain gained. Does it really represent the best life for human beings?

In thinking like this, people are using a notion of natural needs, which coincides pretty closely with that of what Tinbergen has called a major instinct in animals.[5] The objection to keeping a wolf in conditions where he cannot move about freely, or a baby monkey in solitude, is basically just the same as that to keeping a human child in similar conditions.

Let us go back, then, to considering how these major instincts should be conceived in animals. They can be thought of as simply the instincts found at the extreme end of the spectrum which leads from closed to open. A hidebound, fixed hunting pattern is gradually exchanged, in the course of evolution, for a much freer one, and we end up with a flexible 'hunting instinct'. But even at the start of the process, it was sense to describe the creature as having a *hunting instinct*— which we conceive as a wider, more inclusive programme with a number of slots for particular kinds of cues, some of them already specified (such as darkness or noise), some to be gathered from experience, and some providing merely for general exploration and searching, for an *interest* of a particular kind.

Thus the explanatory job done by the notion of an instinct changes radically over the spectrum from closed to open. When we see an animal doing something complex and unfamiliar, we ask 'what's it doing?' If the answer merely names a closed instinct, we are not much the wiser. But we do learn that the behaviour is not—as we might have thought— the result of training, or of individual whim, nor, for instance, of disease or brain damage. The answer, 'That's a closed instinct with them, a fixed action pattern', tells us that it is what all normal members of that species do, *untrained*, and in just that way. If we make normal biological assumptions, this implies something more—namely an inherited neurological mechanism, and an evolutionary history of advantage strong enough to produce that mechanism. This kind of answer is hardly trivial, but it is still thin. It is the kind of answer given when observers are—rather unusually—stuck at the point of recording a common piece of behaviour which they do not yet understand at all. Understanding it means supplying the context; fitting that detailed action into its place within a major instinct. The action, it turns out, is part of hunting, or threatening, or the care of the young. The answer is now much more useful. It tells us the significance of the action, and we have gained a much better idea what more to expect.

Skinner misses this point with his usual instructive thoroughness, calling instinct a 'flagrant example of an explanatory fiction'. He says: 'If the 'instinct' of nest-building refers only to the observed tendency of certain kinds of birds to build nests, it cannot explain why the birds build nests.'[6] It does, however, explain it, first by excluding training, individual invention, disease etc., then by directing attention to the factors (neurological, evolutionary and genetic) known to determine such innate tendencies in detail. But the much commoner and more fertile use of the term is where the particular instinct named is less obvious—where we ask 'why are the gulls pulling up that grass?' and are told that they do that as part of nest-building. This is more instructive still when they don't actually go on to build nests with it, but are only engaged in intention-movements or displacement activities. That action would probably look completely mysterious to someone quite ignorant of gulls. To explain it, we must refer it to its context, namely, the nest-building instinct. Nor is this suggested explanation one which merely says 'all gulls do that'. They need not. The explanation would still hold even for an action which no gull had even done before, such as pulling at the electric flex abandoned by some engineers. What all gulls do is something different (nest-building) to which grass-pulling bears a relation which is understandable once you know how instincts in general work. There is plenty of this kind of thing in human life too, so we need to consider it. To assign a general motive to human conduct is to explain it in just the same way as is done by naming a major instinct. An act (say, a grant to a research institute) which might have been due to scientific curiosity, loyalty, or prudence, turns out to be due to the spirit of competition. Saying this is not making unverifiable references to a mysterious entity, nor to a fishy, subjective sensation as a cause; it is placing it in a wide context in the agent's life. The context supplies the meaning.

I have been attacking my first question—about the specificity of instincts—by saying that a large range of answers is possible. 'Instincts' do not, any more than 'communications' or 'causes' all have to be equally specific. They range from the closed and fully detailed to the wide open. And the more specific ones are grouped within wider patterns, which can be called major instincts. Behaviourists, in rejecting instincts, seem to have had in mind chiefly closed instincts, rigid insect-like patterns. They have not been much interested in wider patterns like sex, fear, play, dominance, curiosity. They have hardly troubled even to deny that such patterns are a fixed feature of the human scene. They have simply taken them for granted as the framework within which cultural variations could be charted. On the other hand, psycho-analytic thinkers, who do use the word instinct,[7] have been chiefly interested in these wider patterns, and particularly in widening the widest of them. Freud saw his task as one of simplifying, of somehow 'reducing' complex phenomena to a few basic forces, and the fewer the better. Speaking of the early days of psycho-analysis, he remarked severely that 'everyone assumed the existence of as many instincts, or "basic instincts" as he chose, and juggled with them like the ancient Greek natural philosophers with their four elements'.[8] He then related with satisfaction how psycho-analysis had succeeded in reducing the number. The trouble, however, does not lie in the number, but in the fact that these Ionian Greeks were not clear what, in detail, they meant by an element, what facts would count as evidence for or against something's being one. And this was just the situation of psychologists about instincts. The implied parallel with chemistry shows how little the number matters. Modern chemists have ended up with a much greater number of elements than the Greeks, but a clear and definite notion of what is meant by an element. By contrast, psychological writers who have claimed to reduce all human motives to one —power, self-preservation, pleasure or what not—have always reduced the number of motives at the cost of expanding the meaning of these chosen terms and finally destroying their explanatory force. What all motives have in common is simply that they are motives, that they move people. But that fact is scarcely exciting enough to sell books.

I am by no means writing off the work at which Freud excelled—the detecting of connections between our particular motives, which will finally reveal one general constitution. I think it of the first importance, and it is worth noticing how often people who claim to dismiss Freud as unscientific make use of these connective schemes, which have passed into our common pool of thought. But such connecting can only be useful where it is informative, where many possible groupings are seriously considered, and positive, empirically detectable marks are recognized which can indicate one answer rather than another. Anyone who 'reduces' all motivation to, for example, power, pleasure or self-preservation thereby makes those words meaningless; they are usable only where they point a contrast. It is a very interesting fact about Freud that he never, in all his changes of view, accepted such a monistic answer, though he was certainly working in the debunking tradition that had common done so. He always recognized the reality of inner conflict. He saw sex as genuinely standing over against some other motive or motives. But this usually appeared to him as a simple two-sided relation, so that the next question was; if sex was the good guy, who were its enemies? Freud identified them successively as hunger, the reality principle, self-preservation, the ego instincts and the death wish, altering the notion of sex (or eros) as he did so. He always, however, conceived these other motives or instincts as somewhat negative, as essentially devices for protecting the ego from interference, unprovided with the vital charge of pleasure which was characteristic of sex. He tended to view all pleasure as by definition sexual, so that the word 'sexual' too became diluted. It followed that eventually (in *Beyond the Pleasure Principle* and still more in *Civilization and its Discontents*) he unveiled the non-sexual instincts as a dreary and negative crew, subsumed under the heading of destructiveness—the death-wish and aggressiveness conceived merely as the death-wish's outward-turning form. The word instinct therefore had for Freud a peculiar though quite familiar limitation. He does not apply it to all natural human motives, but only to certain specially alarming and disruptive one, some sexual, some destructive. For him, instinct and culture were by definition opposed, so that the immensely strong natural motives which nourish culture in every human community had to be ignored or deviously explained as pieces of calculation—even though many of them are quite strongly present in non-calculating animals. He wrote off as illusory all that instinctive sociability which is both an obvious basis of civilization and the cement of life for other social animals. He treated all non-sexual association as a substitute-formation; ('Love with an inhibited aim was in fact originally fully sensual love, and it is so still in man's unconscious')[9] and he therefore took no interest in instinctive patterns which quite evidently serve it, such as talking, greeting, playing, dancing and co-operating generally. Indeed every active, outgoing impulse was highly mysterious on his system, and they usually got explanations like that which he gives for curiosity:[10]

The instinct for knowledge or research . . . cannot be counted among the elementary instinctual components, nor can it be classed as exclusively belonging to sexuality. Its activity corresponds on the one hand to a sublimated manner of obtaining mastery, while on the other it makes use of the energy of scopophilia. The instinct for knowledge in children . . . is in fact possibly aroused by [sexual problems].

There is certainly something impressive in Freud's persistent defence of what he took to be the underprivileged and neglected instincts. In resisting Jung's and Adler's proposals to take other and more obvious motives seriously, he exclaimed:[11]

The truth is that these people have picked out a few cultural overtones from the symphony of life and have once more failed to hear the mighty and primordial melody of the instincts.

But it is not clear that shutting one's eyes and squatting on the floor in the brass section is the best way to do this either. Partiality is a blind guide. As he himself remarked when he eventually admitted aggression as an independent instinct, 'I can no longer understand how we can have overlooked the ubiquity of non-erotic aggressivity and destructiveness'.[12] Enlightenment shouldn't stop there.

Anyone who starts off with a determination to reduce all motivation to a single source, and who chooses a fairly powerful and undervalued motive for his purpose, can make a case as good as Freud's. Nietzsche's programme was no wilder; it was only less industriously carried through:[13]

Assuming, finally, that we succeeded in explaining our entire instinctual life as the development and ramification of one basic form of will (of the will to power, as I hold); assuming that one could trace back all the organic functions to this will to power, including the solution of the problem of generation and nutrition (they are one problem)—if this were done, we would be justified in defining *all* effective energy unequivocally as *will to power*.

This business of psychological reduction has three main forms, which differ a good deal in detail. They get lumped together because all of them, but especially the first two, are well-known ways of unmasking humbug, and this has been a prime concern of reducers. Reducing many desires to one can mean showing that they are either:

1. desires to bring about the same end, the same later event, or
2. desires to gratify the same kind of taste, or
3. forms of the same general desire, parts of the same whole.

Humbug in its simplest mood is caught by pattern (1). This occurs when it proclaims its deep solicitude about the under-privileged in order to get an important contract. Humbug in a rather subtler mood is caught by pattern (2); this occurs when, denied the open enjoyment of fornication, it makes do with public executions and whores whipped naked through town at the cart's tail. Hume and Hobbes specialized in exposing the first kind, Freud and Nietzsche in the second.

Where we actually are dealing with humbug, both these methods are quite satisfactory. The difficulty arises in applying them where we are not. It is nonsense to suggest that humbug is universal, that all or even most human desires are always fraudulently misrepresented. Whom would this fool? More puzzling still, how would anyone know what lie to tell? Humbug is defined by its difference from straightforward behaviour; if there is no straightforward behaviour to imitate, dishonesty means nothing. Faced with such problems, reducers grow more subtle. They move over to pattern three and say, rather, that the various desires are forms, genuinely distinct but related, of a single wide desire. For instance, if the general desire is for pleasure, tastes may vary; some enjoy the pleasure of wine, others of pop music, while others again just happen to prefer giving up everything for their friends or sitting in a cold damp cell waiting to get executed.[14] Anyone who wants to do something has got to take pleasure in it in *some* sense. This sort of view is not silly but it is a bit thin and disappointing; the original insight seems diluted. We have not succeeded in proving that martyrs are actually always plotting to make money by selling their memoirs, or even that they are all masochists or exhibitionists. We feel that the mountain of reductive effort ought to have given us a more impressive animal than this.

A reduction like the one which Freud suggested for curiosity could only be substantial and impressive if it worked by pattern (1) or (2). But pattern (1) is clearly unsuitable. Curiosity cannot just be a means to sexual orgasm; it is not obviously a means to it at all. Pattern (2) is Freud's favourite. When he says that curiosity 'makes use of the energy of scopophilia' he seems to be answering the question usually put in terms of *drive*—namely the question why it is done *at this intensity*. Having already assumed that all the power available is owned either by sex or the ego, he rejects the obvious answer, 'because curiosity is itself a strong natural motive' and substitutes his *a priori* answer. Taken literally in this way as a piece of mental hydraulics, the argument is fanciful and vacuous. There are simply no inner reservoirs or power-stations for us to inspect. But what he actually means is not vacuous at all. It is substantial and empirical, it can be verified, and in this case it is wrong.

Sexual arousal can be provoked by activities which are not overtly sexual, and this is not a fanciful point but an empirical one. An activity which regularly gives people erections etc. has a sexual importance for them, and the conversation of somebody like Iago is as plain an indication of displaced sexual motivation as red litmus paper is of acid. The question is only; is this sort of indication quite generally and necessarily present when people are curious? Or again, if we look at his other, more Nietzschean, explanation of curiosity as 'a sublimated manner of obtaining mastery', do we actually find—not just sometimes but always—that behaviour characteristic of dominance is present? We must deal, not just with the question about intensity, but with the question why *this* is done rather than something else; what is it done *as*? To answer such questions demands a knowledge of the kinds of activity open to a given species, and of the characteristic marks of each. The answer that it is done as a part of sexual activity has to be one of a range of possible answers, for each of which distinct marks can be named. Among these there must be conceivable a set which actually *would* locate it 'among the elementary instinctual components', that is, as done in some sense 'for its own sake'. What does this possibility amount to? What would the marks look like?

Curiosity is a motive widely found in the higher animals as well as in men. This gives us very good opportunities for checking its connection with sex, since (a) animals are not restrained by modesty from expressing their sexual interest openly, and (b) many animals become capable of strong sexual arousal only at certain definite seasons; at other times the hormones for it simply are not present. We ought therefore to find them showing strong curiosity in their sexual seasons and not otherwise, and showing it primarily about each other's sexual activities. But we do not find this. Moreover, animals do not get into the situation which Freud thought produced the intensity of scopophilia (or voyeurism), namely, that of being frustrated and forbidden to watch sexual activity. In spite of this, curiosity is often a very strong motive with them, so strong that predators can sometimes even make use of it to catch, for example, birds and rabbits by acting in some strange and striking manner. This so much interests the proposed prey that they positively gather round to watch. Nor is this interest in new phenomena 'a sublimated manner of obtaining mastery', since they do not normally or necessarily go on to do so. Once they place the new phenomenon, or merely grow used to it, curiosity is satisfied. A desire to use or master it can certainly follow, but the characteristic behaviour is distinct.

Curiosity, in fact, is as evidently independent a motive as any in animals. For any species, it has a characteristic behaviour pattern, so that an experienced observer can tell by plain marks whether the creatures in question are merely curious, or are also, for example frightened, sexually interested, threatening or hungry. Moreover, its distinct evolutionary advantage is obvious, and has nothing to do with sex. It springs from the point mentioned earlier, that the more advanced and flexible species can change their habits, and need to know when it will be necessary or useful to do so. They must explore. They need for this a general readiness to be interested in new objects and enquire about them instead of ignoring them or taking flight. Intelligent 'non-specialist' species do a great deal of this investigation; it comes to its peak in canids and primates, and most of all in man. And we must make a more general observation here. *There is not in animals any sign at all of a system like Freud's or Nietzsche's, whereby any major motive subsumes or rules the rest.*[15] It is of the first importance for an animal to be able to move easily between the main functions of its life—between feeding and mating, rearing the young, cleaning itself, fleeing from danger, investigating objects, quarrelling, finding territory and all the rest of it, as the appropriate occasion arises. To have a dictatorial motive, monopolizing the creature's interest and absorbing the energy needed for other activities would be suicidal.

Freud and Nietzsche were saying something real and important, but the language of reduction cannot express it. They were both struck by the way in which motives can become entangled, can converge to produce unexpected results. In particular, each was struck by the way in which a certain strong motive which people fear and undervalue can influence conduct which is supposed to have nothing to do with it. What they should have noticed was that they were on to something much more general, something which had nothing to do with the respectability of the motive concerned. Two motives, both of them respectable and acknowledged, can combine in just the same confusing way, so that we are uncertain which is in charge, and so can two disreputable motives. This does not mean that they are not 'originally' distinct. In dealing with such problems, we will get nowhere by assuming that there is somewhere a single substratum which will supply 'the secret', nor indeed that there *is* such a secret, a hidden solution available only to the learned, which will suddenly reveal that all the obvious, glaring facts of our emotional life are simply a misleading froth, that the whole truth lies elsewhere. The notion that psychology is essentially esoteric, that common sense is almost by definition wrong about it, is most unplausible. Common sense must have the last laugh here. For practical purposes, people have to understand each other's motives to some extent, and have been practising that art as long as our species has existed: animals do it too. Certainly they often fail, but their cumulative wisdom makes the only possible starting-point for theory.

I conclude this hasty sketch by returning to the questions from which we started:

1. How specific are innate tendencies? I have answered that, both in humans and other animals, they vary. Some are highly specific and 'closed'; others much more open and general. And the general ones provide the explanatory terms which we need if we are to understand both the closed ones (which may be few in the human case) and the original, invented activities by which individuals implement the wider patterns. To explain an act *is* to bring it under such a general, natural motive. This explanatory function helps us to deal with the other two questions:

2. How are these tendencies distinguished from one another? How individuated or counted?

If the concepts of motive are to do their explanatory job, they must not be so wide as to become vacuous, but must still be wide enough to give a useful range of comparison. The disadvantage of tracing all action to (say) the will to power, like Nietzsche, is that one can then no longer meaningfully attribute a particular act to ambition. On the other hand, simply to say 'he did it because it is the kind of thing his father does' is too narrow; we need to know his attitude to his father before this gives an explanation. Obviously, in different contexts and different cultures the range covered by useful explanatory concepts will vary greatly. But this variation is not infinite. People can often interpret successfully the motives of those acting in other cultures, sometimes even more successfully than those nearby. Poetry can be exported. And anthropologists do not hesitate to explain the unfamiliar behaviour they record by reference to a range of basic motives which they rightly take to be available everywhere.

Is a basic set of these really given? Animal examples do

supply some evidence of distinct centres in the brain, governing whole ranges of behaviour appropriate to particular
motives—rage, hunger, sex.[16] It seems reasonable to expect
that this holds for people too, in which case the basic set is
indeed given. There is nothing alarming about this, since the
set is of course the one appropriate to the species, not a
standard mammalian issue, and, as we have seen, acts can
flow from a convergence of two or more motives at various
strengths and variously combined. Moreover of course, we
recognize these motives in the first place by observing the
behaviour that manifests them, not by dissecting the brain. I
have suggested curiosity as a case of a motive which must be
recognized as distinct, because the attempt to reduce its
characteristic behaviour to other terms is a failure. In such
cases, what brings the distinct motive to our attention is
usually conflict—as here, when curiosity makes people and
other animals lose their sense of danger. This way of thinking
commits us already to an answer to our last question—3.
What is the relation between these tendencies? Should they be
conceived as distinct atoms or as part of a given structure?
When we use general motives as alternative explanations of
conduct, we are already treating them as parts of a given
structure. Atomism is not an option. We could not start to
discriminate betwen anger and ambition, habit and jealousy
as possible motives for an act unless we had an idea of the
framework within which they work, of the kind of total
character to which they must all belong. However obscure the
idea of the whole may be in detail, its general shape is
essential for explanation. And we do have that idea. No doubt
if we ourselves did not also exemplify it—if we were members
of an alien species with a quite different pattern of motives—
we would have found it very hard to construct such a scheme.
But this is a piece of bad luck which we do not have and need
not imitate. We approach the problems of human psychology
as humans, and it seems a pity to waste that advantage.

NOTES

The Human Heart and Other Organs

1 See for instance, on the central question of causality, *Causal Powers*, by R. Harré and E. H.Madden (Basil Blackwell 1975). On the sense-datum business, *Sense and Sensibilia* by J. L. Austin (Clarendon Press 1962). On mind and matter, *The Concept of Mind* (Hutchinson 1949) and *Dilemmas* (C.U.P. 1964) by G. Ryle. On ethics, *Moral Notions*, by J. Kovesi (Routledge & Kegan Paul 1967) and *Contemporary Moral Philosophy* by G. J. Warnock (Macmillan 1967). On everything, L. Wittgenstein, *Philosophical Investigations* (Basil Blackwell 1953).

2 See *Causal Powers* and many other works by Rom Harré. Also T. S. Kuhn, *The Structure of Scientific Revolutions*. (Chicago 1970), and Konrad Lorenz, *Behind the Mirror* (Methuen 1977).

3 See his rather desperate note, published as an Appendix to the *Treatise of Human Nature*, p. 633 of the Selby-Bigge edition (O.U.P. 1978).

4 I have pointed out some of the strange consequences of this in 'The Neutrality of the Moral Philosopher', *Proceedings of the Aristotelian Society*, Supplementary vol. 48 (1974), and in chapter 9 of my *Beast and Man* (Harvester Press 1979 and Methuen University Paperback).

5 *Language, Truth and Logic*, chapter 6 (Gollancz 1936).

6 *Ethics* (Pelican 1954).

7 *Facts and Values* (Yale 1963).

8 *The Language of Morals* (Oxford 1952) and *Freedom and Reason* (Oxford 1963).

9 *Principia Ethica* (Cambridge 1948) pp. 45–54, and my *Beast and Man* pp. 155–158.

10 See *Beast and Man*, chapter 11, 'On Being Animal as Well as Rational'. The position I deploy there, and in the present section, is in some ways parallel to that—or those—which Lawrence Kohlberg develops in his lively and stimulating article 'From Is To Ought; How to Commit the Naturalistic Fallacy and Get Away With It', in T. Mischel (ed.) *Cognitive Development and Epistemology*, New York (Academic Press 1971). Kohlberg's objections to relativism, behaviourism and anti-naturalism are not unlike mine, though the strategy by which he resists them is different. I have not found it possible to discuss his views without complicating my argument unduly, but I am glad to see them.

11 *Treatise of Human Nature* Book 1, part IV, section vii. Compare his confident and optimistic tone in the Introduction to the same book. A

more moderate sceptical position appears in the later *Enquiry concerning the Human Understanding*, § xii.

12 *Philosophical Papers* (Allen & Unwin 1959).

13 See *Beast and Man* p. 357, note.

Freedom and Heredity

1 The point I want to make in this article is so general that to pick out particular authors here would be invidious and unhelpful. An excellent introduction to the issues involved may be found in *The IQ Controversy; Critical Readings*, N. J. Block and Gerald Dworkin (eds), (Pantheon 1977). On equality, Peter Singer has developed, much more fully, an approach similar to the one I indicate here in his *Practical Ethics* (C.U.P. 1979).

2 *Existentialism and Humanism*, trans. P. Mairet (Eyre Methuen 1948–73), p. 28.

3 See his *Beyond Freedom and Dignity* (Cape 1972).

4 See his *Essay on Liberty*, chapter 3, 'Of Individuality as one of the elements of well-being'. This whole chapter, the seed-bed of modern libertarian thought, depends on the idea of human nature, which it often explicitly mentions. The metaphors here noted may be found on pp. 117, 120 and 127 of the Everyman Edition.

Creation and Originality

1 See pp. 91–97 and Kant, *The Moral Law*, p. 76.

2 Existentialism and Humanism, trans. P. Mairet (Eyre Methuen 1948–73), p. 54.

3 *Republic* 460–463.

4 *Nicomachean Ethics* book 1 chapter 7, book X chapters 5–7.

5 *Existentialism and Humanism* pp. 32–33.

6 *Critique of Judgment*, trans. J. C. Meredith (O.U.P. 1952–73), p. 168.

Moore on the Ideal

1 In *Mind* for 1912.

2 See Chapter 6, p. 90.

3 *Nicomachean Ethics* book 10, chapters 6–8.

4 In 1925, published in his *Philosophical Papers* (Allen & Unwin 1959).

5 See *Principia Ethica*, index, s.v. Mill. This particular depressing passage is on pp. 71–3; it refers to Mill's remarks in the opening pages of chapter IV of *Utilitarianism*.

6 For its whole fascinating history, see W. Gaunt, *The Aesthetic Adventure* (Jonathan Cape 1945).

The Objection to Systematic Humbug

1 See the paper on 'The Nature of Moral Philosophy' in his *Philosophical Studies*, p. 316.
2 *Utilitarianism* ch. 2, p. 17 (Everyman edition).
3 See a good recent discussion by Bernard Williams in *Utilitarianism For and Against*, J. J. C. Smart and B. Williams (C.U.P. 1973), ch. 5 of his contribution.
4 See *Thought and Action* (Chatto & Windus 1965) pp. 119, 216–222 and 245–250. Also his earlier paper 'Logic and Appreciation' in *Aesthetics and Language*, ed. W. Elton (O.U.P. 1954).
5 *Existentialism and Humanism*, trans. P. Mairet (Eyre Methuen 1948–73) p. 41.
6 I have discussed this matter more fully in my book *Beast and Man*, (Harvester Press 1979, Methuen paperback) especially in chapter 11.
7 See a very interesting discussion of phrases like 'evil be thou my good' by Professor G. E. M. Anscombe in *Intention* (Blackwell 1957), § 39–40.
8 See Chapter 1 of the *Groundwork of the Metaphysic of Morals*, translated by H. J. Paton under the title of *The Moral Law* (Hutchinson 1969). All page references to Kant henceforward are to this book, except where otherwise stated.
9 *Utilitarianism* pp. 4 and 49, Everyman edition.
10 Martin Buber, *I and Thou* p. 28 (T. & T. Clark, Edinburgh 1958).
11 See e.g. Epictetus, Dissertations III, xxic, 1.36; Marcus Aurelius *Meditations* V.34, VII.15,26; VIII.47.
12 *Agamemnon* 177. The word is *pathos*.
13 See for instance the passages which Paton has collected in a paper called 'Kant on Friendship', *Proc. British Acad.* XlII, 1956.
14 See (or rather hear) Monteverdi, *The Coronation of Poppaea*. And, on the whole issue of unearned value, papers called 'Moral Luck' by B. Williams and T. Nagel, *Proc. Aristotelian Soc.* 1976.
15 Paton translates, 'Reverence is properly awareness of a value which demolishes my self-love'. But 'demolishes' cannot be right. It is irreconcilable with Kant's clearly stated acceptance of the necessary function of self-love on p. 85 and elsewhere. L. W. Beck in his admirable translation (entitled *Foundations of the Metaphysic of Morals*, Bobbs-Merrill 1959) follows the older Abbott version in translating the word 'thwarts', which seems a perfectly satisfactory rendering for '*abbruch thun*'. Kant does not need extra trouble.
16 pp. 66–7, note. Kant further developed the very fruitful idea that a situation could conceptually demand a certain emotional response in the Critique of Judgment, where he said that Beauty was a *ground* of delight to all men, and not just a cause of it. Though struck by the

strangeness of this, he insisted that it must be right. See the Meredith translation, p. 50 (O.U.P. 1952).

17 See N. Dent, 'Duty and Inclination' in *Mind*, October 1974 for a more thorough demolition of the idea that there must be something false or unnatural about deliberately changing one's feelings.

18 See R. M. Hare, *The Language of Morals* (O.U.P. 1960) p. 176.

19 For the sort of circle which arises here, see his *Nicomachean Ethics*, bk. 2.1 and even more interestingly, at bk. 3.5 for the effect of this on our responsibility for being the kind of people that we are.

20 Kant's *Theories of Ethics*, trs. T. K. Abbott, p. 313.

Is 'Moral' a Dirty Word?

1 P. Foot, 'When is a Principle a Moral Principle?', *Proc. Arist. Soc.* Supplementary volume, 1954.

2 P. Foot, 'The Philosopher's Defence of Morality' *Philosophy* 1952.

3 P. Foot, 'Moral Arguments', *Mind* 1958.

4 Boswell, *Life of Johnson*, Everyman edition Vol. II p. 28.

5 Shelley took this line in his *Defence of Poetry*.

6 Boswell, *Life of Johnson* Vol. II p. 37.

7 ibid. Vol. II p. 526.

8 ibid. Vol. I p. 477.

9 ibid. Vol. I p. 246.

10 Johnson, *Life of Savage* (O.U.P. 1971) p. 74.

11 Moore. *Principia Ethica* Ch. 1 Sec. 6.

12 Boswell. Vol. 1 p. 275.

13 Kant. *Groundwork of the Metaphysic of Morals* Ch. 1 p. 64.

14 ibid. Ch. II, p. 73.

15 Mill. *Essay on Liberty* Ch. IV (Everyman ed. p. 138).

16 Mill. *Utilitarianism* Ch. V (Everyman ed. p. 45).

17 Plato. *Republic* 357a–368a.

18 Hare. *Language of Morals* pp. 52 and 176.

19 Moore, 'The Nature of Moral Philosophy', *Philosophical Studies*, p. 314.

20 See a most interesting discussion in Julius Kovesi's *Moral Notions*, chapter 1, sec. 4.

21 Mill, *Utilitarianism* chapter 2, Everyman Edition p. 20.

22 See Kovesi, *Moral Notions*, chapter 1, sec. 1.

23 *Nicomachean Ethics* book X, chapter 6.

24 *Essay on Liberty* chapter 3.

25 *Genealogy of Morals* chapter 1.

26 *Iliad* VI. 440–494.

27 *Genealogy of Morals*, chapter 2, opening passage.

The Game Game

1 *Revue Internationale de Philosophie*, no. 70 (1964) pp. 398–412. Reprinted in *Theories of Ethics*, ed. Philippa Foot (O.U.P., 1967) along with John Searle's article 'How to Derive Ought from Is', originally published in the *Philosophical Review* Vol. 73 (1964) pp. 32–58, to which it is an answer.
2 A. R. Manser, 'Games and Family Resemblances', *Philosophy* (1967). H. Khatchadourian, 'Common Names and Family Resemblances' in *Philosophy and Phenomenological Research*, Vol. XVIII (1957–8), reprinted in *Wittgenstein*, George Pitcher (ed.) (Macmillan Modern Studies in Philosophy, 1968.)
3 See an excellent paper by Caroline Loizos on 'Play Behaviour in Higher Primates' in *Primate Ethology*, Desmond Morris (ed.) (Weidenfeld & Nicolson 1967.)
4 See Desmond Morris, *The Naked Ape*, p. 32, also Caroline Loizos, op. cit. pp. 185 and 214.
5 For examples see my *Beast and Man* pp. 247–8 on Dance, and Desmond Morris's admirable book *The Biology of Art* (Methuen, 1962).
6 Ruth Benedict *Patterns of Culture* (Routledge & Kegan Paul 1935–68) pp. 95, 123 and 115.

The Notion of Instinct

1 *The Behaviour of Organisms*, p. 7 (Appleton-Century 1938)—a passage full of instructive mistakes.
2 See G. Ryle, *The Concept of Mind*, chapter 2, *Knowing How and Knowing That* (Hutchinson's University Library 1949).
3 Comparing them to 'generosity, gout or kidney disease' transmitted in families (Letter xxxviii).
4 In 'Behaviour Programs and Evolutionary Strategies', *American Scientist* 62 (1974).
5 N. Tinbergen, *The Study of Instinct*, chapter V (Oxford 1969).
6 *Science and Human Behavior* p. 157 (Free Press, New York, 1953).
7 Freud's official translators render the somewhat general German word *trieb* by *instinct* rather than *drive* for very good reasons, given in a useful note on pp. xxiv–xxvi of their first volume (Freud's *Complete Psychological Works*, Hogarth Press 1966). Freud's own paper on 'Instincts and their Vicissitudes' (1915) in his *Works* vol. XIV explains his use further. For problems about *drive*, see R. A. Hinde, 'Ethological Models and the Concept of Drive', *British Journal for the Philosophy of Science*, 6 (1956).
8 *Beyond the Pleasure Principle*, p. 51, Complete Works vol. XVIII (Hogarth Press).
9 *Civilization and its Discontents* p. 71 (Hogarth Press 1930).
10 *Three Essays on Sexuality*, essay 2, sec. 5, p. 194, *Works* vol. VII (a passage dating from 1915).

11 'On the History Of the Psycho-analytic Movement', *Works* vol. XIV, p. 62.
12 *Civilization and its Discontents*, p. 99.
13 *Beyond Good and Evil*, section 36, trans. M. Cowan (Gateway 1966).
14 For this treatment of the 'kinds' of pleasure, see D. Hume, *Treatise of Human Nature*, Book III, part 1, section 2.
15 See my *Beast and Man*, p. 168.
16 See N. Tinbergen, *The Study of Instinct*, chapter V, section 7 on 'The Neurophysiological Facts', and A. Storr, *Human Aggression*, (Allen Lane 1968) ch. 2, for the situation in people.

Index